ON
HUMAN
DIGNITY

Jürgen Moltmann

ON HUMAN DIGNITY

Political Theology and Ethics

SCM PRESS LTD

Translated from the German by
M. Douglas Meeks

Molton, Jürgen
   On human dignity.
   1. Civil rights——Religious aspects——
   Christianity
   I. Title
   261.7   BT738.15

   ISBN 0-334-01176-0

334 01176 0

First published in Great Britain 1984 by
SCM Press Ltd
26-30 Tottenham Road London N1 4BZ

Typeset in the United States of America and
printed in Great Britain by
Billing & Sons, Worcester

Contents

Part III: Christian Criticism of Religion

Acknowledgments

I am pleased to acknowledge the translation work of Dr. O. C. Dean, Jr., on the essays "Barth's Doctrine of the Lordship of Jesus Christ and the Experience of the Confessing Church," "The Right to Meaningful Work," and "Olympism and Religion," and of Rev. Steven Gehlert on "Church and Israel: A Common Way of Hope?"

The following essays have appeared in English: "America as Dream" in *The Center Magazine* 104 (1977):16; "Christian Faith and Human Rights" in *A Declaration on Human Rights,* ed. A. O. Miller (Grand Rapids: Wm. B. Eerdmans, 1977); "Ecumenical Dialogue on Human Rights" in *Understanding Human Rights,* ed. A. Falconer (Dublin, 1980). The essays of Part II appeared in shorter form in *Following Jesus Christ in the World Today.* Occasional Paper No. 4, Institute of Mennonite Studies Elkhart, Indiana.

M. Douglas Meeks

Introduction

by M. Douglas Meeks

"Dignity" is a difficult word to define. Often it has denoted the honor of rank so that it referred merely to the status of a dignitary. Dignity in this sense is nothing more than a privilege or prerogative or even simply a sense of decorum. Thus interpreted, dignity is a distinction gained by action or status. It will be a property attributed only to select individuals of the human species. But since the Enlightenment "dignity" has increasingly meant the worth of being human. *Dignitas* became so closely associated with *humanitas* as to be construed as a synonym. To be able to say what dignity is would be to describe the fundamental meaning of being human. Thus the loss of dignity and even the very meaning of dignity are issues over which many human beings are wont to fight and willing to die. For this reason, dignity has become the key concept in the worldwide struggle for human rights. But despite the fact that dignity is a word on everyone's lips, it remains elusive.

In the following essays Jürgen Moltmann addresses the question of human dignity from the perspective of Christian theology. Moltmann has been at the forefront of the ecumenical church's work on human rights. Over the last two decades most churches in the world have realized that their ministries of justice and peace have to be carried out in terms of human rights. Simultaneously, however, the world situation has become increasingly dangerous precisely because of deep ideological disagreements over human rights. Three mammoth ideological phalanxes have emerged. The so-called First World has developed the liberal ideology that asserts the right of the individual over against the state. The Second World has championed the Marxist-Leninist emphasis on the rights of society. And finally the Third World has averred the rights of self-development and self-determination of a people's future. Human rights have become the focus of the deadly struggle for supremacy among the world's power blocs.

In each of these ideological approaches human dignity is identified narrowly with only a few dimensions of human life or with a limited number of human rights. The result is that the question of human dignity can be constantly eclipsed by this or that ideological compulsion. Dignity is identified with the private individual's rights in a market society, or with the rights assumed by the state in order to assure social rights, or with a people's right to determine its own future. Dignity defined in any of these ways immediately entails a counter-definition of others as inhuman, not possessing dignity. Thus is born the stuff of enemy pictures. With some despair one can note that the conflict between claims about rights is itself a source of the possible destruction of humanity.

What should be the contribution of Christian theology in this situation? It will first of all join those who refuse narrow, ideological definitions of human dignity as reducible to any specific rights or politico-economic arrangements. Dignity is not bestowed by persons or institutions. It does not derive its meaning from any human action or status. Dignity is rather a given, universally shared reality. It is not itself a moral principle but rather the source of all moral principles. Human dignity is the norm by which all forms of human acting and deciding are to be judged. But these formal judgments do not yet tell us what human dignity is. If Christian theology cannot entertain the identification of human dignity with the interests of some people and nations over against others, neither can it be satisfied with abstract and formalistic definitions of dignity.

By proposing a Christian perspective on human dignity Moltmann intends in these essays a contribution to the wider debate on human rights. Christian theology understands human dignity on the basis of biblical testimonies, the narratives of Israel and Jesus. According to these narratives human dignity is based on God's claim to the creation. Human dignity is grounded in God's creativity, that is, God's power to call everything that is out of the power of the *nihil*. God has the right to everything that exists because God's power for life has brought into being everything in the creation. God's faithfulness to the creation is the heart of human dignity. The concrete form of God's faithfulness to the creation is God's infinite readiness for suffering for the sake of the life of the creation. Christologically stated, the price God pays for God's right to all creatures is "the Lamb slain from the foundation of the world." Human dignity, then, is God's claim on human beings. It is not something created by human declaration. Human rights spring from human dignity and not vice versa.

Human dignity, however, requires human rights for its embodiment, protection, and full flowering. Human rights are the concrete, indefeasible claim of human dignity. Without human rights, human dignity cannot be historically realized in action. The great value of the first two essays is Moltmann's demonstration of how fundamental human rights are grounded in God's right and how fundamental human rights are necessary to prevent the destruction of human dignity. The remaining essays are organized around three major themes that correspond to the way human rights are often distinguished: basic human *needs* (which Moltmann relates primarily to the human being's creation as the image of God), human *freedom* (related to liberation through the incarnation of the crucified risen Christ), and access to human *community*, especially religious community (related to the eschatological coming of God's kingdom).

From the perspective of the biblical testimonies human rights are grounded in God's creation of the human being in God's image. To be created as a human being means to be commissioned to represent God's will to the creation. This commission is what distinguishes the human being from the rest of creation and what constitutes being human. Human rights are whatever human beings need in order to keep this commission. Human responsibility, then, precedes and gives rise to human rights. God's right to claim the human being's life in God's own mission of making the creation live against the powers of death, evil, and sin is the ground of every human being's claim to whatever it takes to fulfill this commission, namely, what it takes to be human. The basic rights that are needed for the human being to be God's steward are rights to food, shelter, clothing, health care, education, and so on. These rights cannot be denied persons without denying their humanity.

Second, the biblical testimonies speak of the freedom of the human being that comes from God's suffering love incarnated in Jesus Christ. The human being has a right to be free from all tyrannies of political and economic domination as well as religio-cultural systems that distort life and prevent one from responsibly giving one's own life to others just as God has given God's life away in the cross of Jesus Christ. The rights that are grounded in God's gracious liberating work in the world are the personal rights to the freedom of political participation (freedom of speech, press, assembly, etc.) and freedom of the public profession of religious belief.

Third, the biblical tradition points to the coming sovereignty of God's righteousness. The human being has a duty and therefore a right to be related to the world that God loves and that God will redeem. Responsibility to the wholeness and health of God's world and to the coming generations requires rights to those relationships that are necessary for a person to be related to the world and to God's comprehensive promise to the world. The rights that come from the approach of God's kingdom and our responsibility to it are rights to found, have access to, and participate in a family, in communities, and in associations.

According to Moltmann, then, human dignity is based in God's redeeming history with the world. Human rights reflect what God is doing and requiring to meet basic human needs, to free human beings from their idolatry, and to bring human beings into communal relationships, including relationships to past and future generations. This conception of human dignity and human rights provides the framework for the political theology which is fleshed out in these essays.

The chapter on "The Right to Meaningful Work" functions in the area of basic human needs and points to the way human dignity can be lost in the dimension of human work. Whether work is denigrated as the means of providing the necessities of life and thus identified as forced labor or exalted as the means of gaining self-worth or of actually creating one's life and future, work is always a dimension in which human dignity can be distorted and destroyed. From a biblical perspective on dignity Moltmann redefines work on the basis of God's calling to human beings to participate in God's struggle for life against death in the creation. The dignity of human beings does not depend on work, but yet the human being has a right to work as a way of presenting his or her life to God, participating in community, and fulfilling God's commission. The human need for work transcends economic systems and is ultimately based on God's claim to the human being.

The four essays of the second section focus on the questions of freedom and power in the church's relationship to the state. The apocalyptic view of history in the Lutheran two-kingdoms doctrine is set over against the doctrine of the lordship of Jesus Christ, especially as articulated in the Barmen Confession (1934). As an alternative to these two extremes Moltmann develops an eschatological political theology. This alternative position is then tested in terms of the new religious situations of freedom and power in the nuclear age in which human beings for the first time in history have the capacity for destroying the world. Neither the just war theory of the Christian tradition nor the modern liberal and Marxist theories of freedom can adequately address the demonic nature of the doctrine of deterrence and its spiral of unending armaments based on the infinite capacity for threat and counter-threat in human fear. Freedom must have a new interpretation: not just freedom as restraint of the state in favor of the individual or of the individual in favor of the state. Rather, for the sake of the future of the world we must speak of a freedom from whole cultural, social, and religious systems of coercion, that is, a freedom to live defenselessly. Moltmann calls on the left wing of the Reformation to clarify this freedom as an eschatological realism over against the paradoxical realism of the Lutheran and the triumphalist realism of the Reformed ethic.

The last section of the book is unified around the theme of the promise and threat to human dignity represented by religion, especially the messianic religion of Western Christianity. Human dignity is most deeply and thoroughly distorted by religion. Here political ethics is understood to be messianic ethics. The first task of messianic ethics must be the radical criticism of messianism. Moltmann engages in this criticism in five essays dealing with the themes of (1) the messianic dynamic against the old European cultural unity between church and state; (2) the ambivalent messianism of the American dream; (3) the idolatrous messianism of the Olympic religion; (4) the atheistic messianism of the Marxist philosopher Ernst Bloch; and (5) Christianity's relationship to the messianism of Israel, now embodied in a state. The test in each case is whether messianism contains its own principle of self-criticism. If it does not, messianism easily becomes a tool that exchanges one kind of slavery for another.

The messianic element in Western religion and culture has the effect of opening up the future and making present conditions provisional. Because everything is put in suspension by the not-yet-realized, all conditions that destroy human dignity can themselves be negated. But such messianism can have the effect of producing mere optimism and utopia. And, as such, messianism becomes subject to nationalism and chauvinism and prepares the way for definitions of human dignity determined by the strong and excluding the weak. Such messianism is especially susceptible to the pragmatism that construes the whole of life as an experiment. Only the messianism that has the suffering of God at its heart remains a messianism that can nurture human dignity. In Christian terms this means that God is totally invested in the finality of the life and death of God's creatures here and now. Thus the cross is the sign of God's own commitment to human dignity.

PART I

HUMAN RIGHTS

1

Ecumenical Dialogue on Human Rights

Human Rights in the Context of Ecumenical Theology

The ecumenical movement originated at a time almost parallel with the formation of the League of Nations, the international peacework, and the United Nations. It is, therefore, no surprise that as early as 1948 representatives of the World Council of Churches, which was formed in the same year, were collaborators on the *Universal Declaration of Human Rights*. Here above all the Commission of the Churches for International Affairs (CCIA) is to be mentioned. The co-workers of the council and of the commission participated also in the working out, codification, and defense of the later human rights blueprints, especially the 1966 *International Covenants,* which eventually came into effect in 1976 after protracted ratification by the necessary number of thirty-five states. Since then all plenary meetings of the World Council of Churches and most conferences of the world confessional families have had sections which deal with the clarification and enforcement of human rights.

The above-mentioned commission (CCIA) held a conference in 1974 in St. Pölten on "Human Rights and Christian Responsibility," at which representatives from socialist states and the peoples of the Third World took part.[1] This conference represents the high point to date of the ecumenical dialogue concerning human rights. It made a convincing correction to the one-sided Western conceptions in that it drew up a catalog of basic human rights that begins with the right to life. The basis for the present work of the World Council on the theme Human Rights is the detailed recommendation of Section VI of the fifth plenary meeting of the World Council in Nairobi in 1975.[2]

The World Alliance of Reformed Churches decided at its General Assembly in Nairobi (1970) upon a program of study on the theme "Theological Basis of Human Rights and Liberation." After intensive work in all member churches, the present writer was commissioned to do a comprehensive study. This was discussed and accepted at the conference of the Theological Department in London in 1976. Together with recommendations concerning "Theological Guidelines" and "Some Practical Consequences," it was published as *Theological Basis of Human Rights*.[3] At the centenary meeting of the World Alliance of Reformed Churches at St. Andrews in 1977 this *Theological Basis of Human Rights* was officially accepted as the "first step toward an ecumenical 'Christian Declaration on Human Rights.'" Theological cooperation with the World Council, the Lutheran World Federation, the Orthodox church, and the Roman Catholic commissions as well as an ongoing involvement with the problem Human Rights and Politics was also decided upon.

The Lutheran World Federation decided at its assembly in Evian in 1970 on a study concerning human rights. In the summer of 1976 it held a summary conference in Geneva and published the results in 1977[4] under the title *Theologische Perspektiven der Menschenrechte* (Theological Perspectives of Human Rights). The leading writers were Heinz Eduard Tödt and Wolfgang Huber, who published their works on the theme in Germany in 1977.[5] A series of works by individual Lutheran theologians completes the study referred to.[6]

Already in the autumn of 1974, the Roman Synod of Bishops had published a *Message Concerning Human Rights and Reconciliation*.[7] In 1976 the Papal Commission *Justitia et Pax* provided a working paper "The Church and Human Rights."[8]

From the sphere of the Orthodox churches no official declarations on human rights are known to me. Therefore, I can only refer to the above-stated church documents in the following theological reflections.

Looking at the content of these theological declarations and church attitudes in the ecumenical sphere since 1948, one can perceive interesting shifts of emphasis in the treatment.

From 1948 until about 1960 the question of religious freedom stood at the center of church activity and theological work on human rights. Religious freedom, especially in countries with a socialist state ideology but also in countries with state religions, has indeed remained a theme. This is seen in the collaboration of the European Conference of Churches on the Final Declaration on Security and Cooperation of the Summit Conference of Helsinki in 1975 as well as in the dramatic discussion with representatives of the Russian Orthodox church at the fifth plenary meeting in Nairobi in 1975. Nevertheless, it is not the principal theme anymore. Indeed it was already clear at the plenary meeting in Amsterdam in 1948 that freedom of religion and freedom of conscience can only be realized in the context of the other individual rights of freedom and protection. Besides, the church cannot wait with its protest until its own religious freedom is threatened. It is there for the sake of humanity and must raise its voice for the rights of all human beings. The vision from that period of a "responsible society" also shows that fact clearly.

Since about 1960 another theme has pushed itself into the forefront of the ecumenical meetings, at which the voices from the Third World were becoming louder and louder. This theme was the condemnation of racism as a serious violation of fundamental human rights. Here also it was very quickly clear that one cannot separate the phenomena of racist inhumanity from political colonialism and economic exploitation in Africa, Asia, Latin America, and elsewhere. That inseparability means, however, that one has had to learn not to conceive of human rights as "individual freedom" rights anymore. The fourth plenary meeting of the World Council in Uppsala in 1968 recognized that "in the modern worldwide community the rights of the individual are unavoidably tied to the fight for a better living standard for the socially disadvantaged of many nations. Human rights cannot be secured in a world of gross inequality and social conflicts."[9] Thus came to the fore the knowledge that there are economic, social, and cultural human rights about which the history of freedom in Western Europe has had little to say. The *International Covenants* of 1966 also place the "economic and social rights" in the primary position and the "civil and political rights" only in second place. Indeed in what other way shall a human being actualize his or her individual freedom rights if he or she does not find the economic and social possibilities for doing so?

While the Marxists since 1948 have repudiated human rights as bourgeois ideology for the veiling of capitalist exploitation, socialist concepts of human rights have for the first time been introduced and discussed through the *International Covenants* of 1966 and since the 1974 St. Pölten Conference. Indeed it says in the Socialist *Internationale*, "O peoples hear the signals to the last fight: the *Internationale* is fighting for the human right." However, there is still a considerable distance to go in the dialogue between East and West on the way to a common understanding of human rights. Hitherto each has understood human rights differently and contradictorily to the other.

For all that, other priorities are coming once again into the ecumenical human rights discussion from the peoples of the Third World, who are seeking their path to freedom from colonial dependence, cultural alienation, and political suppression. In these countries the interest in freedom of the press or in the right to strike is understandably slight. The right to life and to the means which make continued living possible stands in the forefront. The St. Pölten Report, therefore, just like the Roman Synod of Bishops, places the right to life, to nourishment, and to work at the beginning of the catalog of human rights.

The history of the ecumenical discussion concerning human rights shows a quite striking development from the almost entirely accepted predominance of the Western civil-liberal view of human rights and the social rights of the human community to the eventual perception of the life interests of the Third World. This development went through many tensions and conflicts, which are still by no means overcome. "Religious freedom," "racism," "economic self-reliance" are still catch phrases which point in different directions.

Becoming all the more important is the knowledge of the inner link that holds the individual, social, and life-giving human rights together. Because the concern is with the one human being, with the one human race, and with a shared humanity, one must ask about the thread that holds them inwardly together. Many conferences have contented themselves with drawing up pragmatic catalogs of necessary and desirable human rights. But such simple addition does not help because it does not impede the unfortunately inevitable subtraction that pertains in many situations. Certainly there are priorities which correspond to the different situations in which humanity is suffering. But the priorities which are necessary for action turn into ideology if they are deemed absolute. Priorities do not exclude other things but just defer them for the time being.

Christianity, which has trod a common path in the ecumenical movement, has hitherto preserved its solidarity in the three worlds—and that in spite of their conflicts. Despite everything, there lives in these tensions the common faith. The ecumenical human rights discussion shows the outstanding openness and flexibility of Christians, who must live in such contradictory situations. On account of that, I believe, the further knowledge, development, and advancement of human rights has become the framework of ecumenical politics and ethics. Liberation, development, passive and active resistance, the overcoming of racism, economic aid to developing countries, nuclear reactors, and the building up of a sustainable society are discussed today within the framework of human rights. For church guidelines on political and social matters gain their universal significance only through reference to human rights. Through its relationship to human rights the church becomes the church for the world.

Work on the Theological Basis of Human Rights

Most ecumenical conferences (which, among other things, deal also with human rights) content themselves with drawing up lists of rights which they consider essential for each person's human- ity. The arrangement of the rights on these lists then indicates the priorities—"human rights, which today are especially threat- ened." Thus we find in the St. Pölten Report a six-point list which begins with the "right to life," followed by the "recognition of cultural identity," after which it speaks of "participation in deci- sion processes," "freedom of opinion," "the right to personal dignity," and "freedom of religion." The list of the 1974 Roman Synod of Bishops looks quite similar; after the "right to life" comes the "right to nourishment," socioeconomic rights, politi- cal and cultural rights, and the right to religious freedom. How- ever, it must evidently already have been felt in St. Pölten that it is not enough simply to draw up such checklists of wishes. There- fore, it was said: "All human rights, be they social, economic, religious, or political are interrelated. They must be taken as a whole. The churches should give them equal importance and seek the application of all of them." But how can one conceive of human rights as a whole if one knows only the different lists of them? In what does their unity consist? From where can one grasp them as an entirety?

Here there are two different approaches. Heinz Eduard Tödt and Wolfgang Huber, whom the Lutheran World Federation fol- lows in its 1977 declaration, propose, instead of drawing up lists and priorities, to replace them with an ideal-typical method of viewing all human rights. One can, that is, see three basic ele- ments (*Sachmomente*) in all human rights: they are freedom, equality, and participation. In this triad Tödt and Huber see the ideal basic contours of human rights. They use this figure as a hermeneutical key to the understanding of the plurality of human rights. Thus it becomes possible to define what human right in the singular actually is. Of course, the uncertainty that one cannot know how these three dimensions function in the case of each particular right must be tolerated. Indeed freedom and equality lead to contradiction in most cases, since it is very difficult to actualize both of them simultaneously.

Justitia et Pax and the Reformed *Theological Basis of Human Rights* start out from the distinction between dignity and human rights. Human rights are plural, but human dignity exists only in the singular. Therefore, the dignity of human beings takes precedence over the many rights and duties which are bound up with being human. The dignity of humanity is the one indivisible, inalienable, and shared quality of the human being. The different human rights portray a wholeness because the human being in his or her dignity is a totality. The completeness of the catalogs and lists of human rights is not identical with this totality. The light of totality falls much more from the human being's dignity onto every fragment of his or her human rights.

The *Universal Declaration of Human Rights* of 1948, Article 1, and most political constitutions which establish those human rights as the fundamental rights of the citizens start with this fundamental anthropological distinction between human dignity and human rights. The dignity of the human being is not itself a human right but a source and ground for all human rights, and all human rights promote respect for the singular worth of human beings.

First, we shall follow this distinction. The one, indivisible, inalienable dignity of humanity can be—as just seen—negatively so phrased that human beings of different beliefs and ideologies can agree. That circumstance is an advantage, for a teaching about human rights must be open for all human beings and must itself practice religious freedom. However, one can proceed a step beyond these negative descriptions of the dignity of humanity if one goes into the general condition of being human: Human dignity lies in the fact that each particular human being and all human beings are, in common, human. If this sentence is not to be a tautology, then it presupposes the difference between the existence and the essence of the human being: The human being is a human being, and ought to be a human being. The being-a-human contains his or her humanity initially only as possibility, but not yet as constant reality. With the *hominitas,* the *humanitas* is at stake. It can be actualized, but it can also be blocked. Only of a human being do we say that he or she acts "inhumanly" if he or she violates human rights. With a dog it is not even linguistically possible to say something like this.

So the dignity of human beings consists in this, that they are human and should be human. Their existence is gift and task simultaneously. It presents them with the task of actualizing themselves, their essence, and thus coming into their truth. At this point there is in the Lutheran, the Reformed, and also in the Catholic documents a strange polemic against humanism and the modern personal as well as corporate striving for autonomy. Christian apologetics have again and again in modern European times defamed the will to self-actualization as irreligious, anti-Christian, and revolutionary, as if this were the quintessence of egoism. Against that criticism, what is Christian is the championing of the neighbor's right, the defense of the other, thus the renouncing of one's own rights. Against the modern self-actualization the churches like to place selflessness in love. But the question is, Which self is meant? If one's self is his or her essence as human, then self-actualization has nothing to do with egoism but is one side of the biblical commandment of love: "Love your neighbor as yourself" (it does not say the reverse: "Love yourself as your neighbor"). Love of self is the other side of the love of the neighbor. So without self-actualization there is also no actualization of humanity for others! The laying claim to one's own rights does not require justification through love in the sense, more or less, that one really only wants to be there for others, but it is itself a part of the commandment of love.

In the more close characterizing of the dignity and the essence of the human being the distinguishably Christian contribution of theology must emerge. Christians cannot expect that all people agree with their Christian view of the human being. Therefore, there is here no absolutism of the Christian faith. But all other human beings can expect that Christians both say and show what they think of the dignity of the human being and what they can contribute to the realization of human rights. Thus, there is here the openness of the Christian faith.

St. Pölten was satisfied with a short confession: "It is our conviction that the emphasis of the gospel is on the value of all human beings in the sight of God, on the atoning and redeeming work of Christ that has given to man his true dignity, on love as the motive for action, and on love for one's neighbor as the practical expression of an active faith in Christ. We are members one of another, and when one suffers all are hurt.''

In the declaration of the Roman Synod of Bishops the key sentence reads quite similarly: "The dignity of man has its roots in the fact that every human being is an image and reflection of God. As a result of this all men are equal with one another in their essence. The entire personal unfolding of man is a manifestation of this picture of God in us. . . . The mystery of the incarnation—the Son of God takes on human nature—throws new light upon the picture of man and his dignity as it is accessible to our natural understanding. For it is only in the mystery of the Word-made-flesh that the mystery of man is truly brought to light.''

Most comprehensively of all, the Reformed *Theological Basis* saw the dignity of the human in his or her being in God's image, and unfolded this being in God's image in its important dimensions:

1. The image of God is the human being who co-responds to God.

2. Insofar as human beings co-respond to God, their Creator, they come into God's truth.

3. The human being co-responding to God is the beginning and the end of the history of God with human beings in creation, reconciliation, and salvation.

4. The human being should co-respond to God in his or her relationship to himself or herself. The human being is in this respect a person, and thus he or she has essential rights to freedom.

5. The human being should co-respond to God in his or her relationship to other human beings. Persons are in this respect human beings and thus have essential community rights.

6. The human being should co-respond to God in his or her relationship to nonhuman creation. The human being is destined for jurisdiction over and oneness with the earth and thus has essential economic rights and ecological duties.

7. Finally, the human being should co-respond to God in the succession of generations. The human being is in this respect a

historical being and has corresponding temporal rights and duties in the succession of generations.

Because it is often emphasized on the Lutheran side that the human being's dignity is his or her being an image of God, one can see here a real convergence of all Christian declarations about human rights.

Where do the differences lie and where are there ambiguities?

Theological Differences and
Open Questions

The Reformed-Lutheran Difference. The Reformed *Theological Basis* grounds human rights in human dignity and human dignity in humanity's being an image of God, and the being an image of God in God's right to human beings. It follows therewith the "theological foundation of right" (J. Ellul) and the direction "justification of right" (K. Barth). It sees the human being as the image of God in the federal-theological context of the covenant of God. This mode of substantiation has certainly the disadvantage that it is only acceptable for Christians. But it has the advantage that it motivates and activates Christians for human rights and their enforcement, and furthermore precisely as Christians and not just indirectly.

The Lutheran critique of Tödt and Huber gets underway with the "two kingdoms" doctrine. According to this, human rights are secular phenomena to which Christians can refer not directly as Christians but only indirectly with the help of their "reason illumined by love." They recognize, then, in human rights similarities and analogies to the Christian faith. A "Christian foundation" of human rights is rejected. Nevertheless "the basis from whence we Christians are to deal with and understand the secular human rights should be examined."

Where does the difference lie between one basis and another? Tödt and Huber analyze in the phenomena of human rights "elements of transcendence," which point toward the promises of the gospel. They find "manifest correspondences between the actual elements of the contours of the human right and the basic contents of Christian faith." In this way they should like as theologians to deal with human rights in a critically constructive way, not to legitimate them. It is not easy for an outsider to grasp the real difference between the Lutheran and the Reformed conceptions. Basically, the reflection which "reason enlightened through faith" takes up amounts to the same thing as the "theological foundation" of human rights based on God's right to the human being. The real difference lies presumably in the historical characteristics of the tradition. Since the Puritan revolution, the Reformed churches have had a direct part and therefore also a direct interest in human and civil rights. The Lutheran churches have had to make the effort after the event to relate to something in the emergence of which they have scarcely had any part.

However, the question remains open as to how the particularity of the Christian faith is to be referred and applied to the universal reality of human rights.

The Roman Catholic-Reformed Difference. Here also the prejudgments of the different traditions are operative. In the arrangement of official declarations through *Justitia et Pax,* the Thomistic scheme of nature and grace is distinctly recognizable: "All human beings are distinguished with the same dignity of nature, but it is only in the mystery of the Word of God become flesh that the mystery of the human being truly becomes clear." In the Reformed *Theological Basis* the scheme of sin and grace is visible: "For the Christian world God's right to the human being in this world of sin and inhumanity is manifest through the gospel of Christ. Because the divine right of grace is made known to all human beings through this gospel, the God-given dignity of every human being and of all humanity is simultaneously proclaimed with it."

Both perspectives, properly understood, do not exclude each other. Grace, which nature presupposes, establishes a universal horizon. Grace, which justifies sinners, makes it possible to experience concretely God's justice. In the Reformed declaration one can see the *imago Dei* teaching as a common Christian basis. In the Roman Catholic declaration the central reference is to the "light of the gospel," in which the church acknowledges human rights, and this finds acceptance by Protestant Christians.

The common concentration on the gospel of Christ does not

limit the universalism of human rights, but rather lights up the broadest sphere from the creation of the human being to the completion of human history. To understand this, one must distinguish between the order of things and the order of knowledge. The revelation of God in Christ through the gospel is the way to the knowledge of the dignity of all, and of every human being as the image of God, and to the hope for all humanity and every human being of becoming human in the divine kingdom of freedom. Thus, what is known in faith through revelation is presupposed and unfolded through revelation: creation, on the one hand; fulfillment, on the other.

However, the question remains open here, as to how this knowledge is constituted with a view to human rights.

The Experience of Liberation and the Commitment to Human Rights. In the Roman Catholic declaration the starting point from the perspective of knowledge lies in the explanations of the teaching office of the church, the task of which it is to bear witness to the gospel and to preserve the tradition. Thus, the starting point for the individual Christian is the experience of Christ's church. In the Reformed declaration the starting point lies in the testimonies of Holy Scripture, which make known to all human beings the good news of the justice of God manifest in Christ. Thus, the starting point for the individual Christian is the experience of justification in his or her own faith.

However, there is in fact yet a third starting point which is ever present in one way or another in the two already mentioned: this is the starting out from one's own life experience. Whether as members of the church of Christ or as believers in Christ, our understanding of humanity and of human rights is stamped with our personal and collective life experience. We experience the inhumanity of a dictatorship, of economic exploitation, of racism, or the destruction of nature insofar as we have to live in it. We experience these states of affairs as "inhuman" if we have been made sensitive through the contrary experience of humanity. Otherwise we would get used to them. We experience suffering due to unfreedom as a conscious pain if and wherever freedom has come nearer. We fashion our views of freedom and humanity according to our hopes and our experiences.

Suffering under racism will lead one to grasp another aspect of human rights than does suffering under ideological dictatorship. And from the Christian perspective, suffering from a world growing ever more divided and hostile even as it grows more interdependent is certainly the experience of the church of Christ and the experience of Christ in one's own faith. But both experiences stand in the context of the real history of oppression and liberation, of inhumanity and humanity. If one were to isolate out of this context the special Christian experience, then this Christian experience would become abstract and would not be communicable anymore. We have learned from liberation theology to begin where we ourselves really exist in our own people. Experience in the praxis of liberation from inhumanity is for Christians and churches the concrete starting point for the commitment to human rights.

The Task of Christian Theology

The task of Christian theology does not lie in presenting once again what thousands of experts, jurists, parliamentarians, and diplomats in the United Nations have already completed. However, Christian theology also cannot allow itself to dispense with the discussion of and the fight for the realization of human rights. In the name of the creation of the human being in the image of God, in the name of the incarnation of God for the reconciliation of the world, and in the name of the coming kingdom of God for the fulfillment of history, the church is charged with responsibility for the humanity of persons as well as for their rights and duties in time. We see the theological contribution of the Christian church in the grounding of the fundamental human rights upon God's right to human beings. The Christian faith has over and above the different rights and duties of humanity to esteem the one indivisible dignity of the human being in his or her life with God—without, in so doing, excluding other religious or humanistic conceptions of human rights.

Christian theology refers to the history of God with human

15

beings on the basis of the biblical testimonies. This history is about the salvation of human beings from their sinful godlessness (Adam) and the liberation from their deathly inhumanity (Cain), and therein about the fulfillment of their original destiny to be the image of God.

In accordance with the Old Testament, theology reflects the liberation of Israel from slavery in Egypt, the covenant of the liberating God with the chosen community, and the rights and duties of the people of God which are laid down in this covenant of freedom. These salvation events—liberation, covenant, and the right of God—are the concrete content of the biblical testimony of the Old Testament, furthermore in this sequence. They have power of guidance for Israel and Christianity in particular, and through both they have exemplary meaning for all human beings and nations. Through justice and peace Israel and the Christian world become the light of nations.

In accordance with the New Testament, theology reflects the liberation of human beings from sin, law, and death through the sending, the sacrifice, and the resurrection of Jesus Christ. Through the role of the crucified Son of God the power of the Evil One is broken. In the Son's Parousia the freedom of the children of God will appear. Liberation through the mediating death of Christ, the new covenant in his blood, and the new rights and duties of the ecclesial community composed of masters and slaves, Jews and unbelievers, men and women (Gal. 3:28) are the concrete content of the biblical witness of the New Testament. Because Christ in his mission, his sacrifice, and his resurrection is the "visible image of the unseen God," human beings in his community become his brothers and sisters and tread the path leading to the fulfillment of their human destiny as the image of God in the world. In the grace of God lies the dignity of the human beings.

Inasmuch as Christian theology reflects the liberation, the covenant, and the right of God according to the biblical testimonies, it discovers also the freedom, the solidarity, and the rights of human beings today. It therefore awakens pain over the present internal and external enslavements of human beings. It calls for commitment to liberation for a life in the dignity, the rights, and

16

the duties of community with God. In a world which is not yet the kingdom of God, Christianity can leave no area of life without the witness to divine liberation, to the covenant of God, and to the dignity of the human being. The biblical witness of liberation, covenant, and the right of God leads to a corresponding praxis of the Christian world.

The universal presupposition of the special history of God with Israel and Christendom lies in the faith that the God freeing and saving them is the Creator of all human beings and things. In God's liberating and saving action, therefore, the original destiny of all human beings is experienced and fulfilled. In the designation of the human being to be the image of God, the right of God to all human beings is expressed. The human rights to life, freedom, community, and self-determination mirror God's right to the human being because the human being is destined to be God's image in all conditions and relationships of life.

The universal goal of Israel's and Christianity's special experiences of God lies in the faith that the God freeing and saving them is the fulfiller of the history of the world and will actualize his right to his entire creation in the kingdom of his glory. God's liberating and saving action in history thus reveals the true future of the human being. Image of God means the full community of God. The human being therefore has a right to future. Human rights mirror the right of the coming God and the future of humanity. The destiny of the human being to be the image of God indicates the indivisible right of God to the human being and, therefore, the irreducible dignity of the human being.

NOTES

1. *Human Rights and Christian Responsibility,* vols. 1–3 (Geneva: WCC—CCIA, 1975). Some of the papers of the conference are published in *Ecumenical Review* 27, no. 2 (1975).

2. David Paton, ed., *Breaking Barriers: The Official Report of the Fifth Assembly of the World Council of Churches,* Nairobi, 23 November–10 December 1975 (London: SPCK, 1976), 119–41.

3. Text and preparatory papers in Allen O. Miller, ed., *A Christian Declaration on Human Rights* (Grand Rapids: Wm. B. Eerdmans, 1977).

4. Jørgen Lissner (pref.), *Theological Perspectives on Human Rights* (Geneva: Lutheran World Federation, 1977). See also Jørgen Lissner and Aren Sovik, eds., *A Lutheran Reader on Human Rights* (Geneva: Lutheran World Federation, 1978).

5. Wolfgang Huber and Heinz Eduard Tödt, *Menschenrechte. Perspektiven einer menschlichen Welt* (Stuttgart: Kreuz Verlag, 1977).

6. J. Baur, ed., *Zum Thema Menschenrechte* (Stuttgart: Calwer Verlag, 1977). T. Rendtorff, "Menschenrechte und Rechtfertigung," in *Der Wirklichkeitsanspruch von Theologie und Religion*, ed. D. Henke (Tübingen, 1976), 161–74. W. Schweitzer, "Bericht," *Zeitschrift für Evangelische Ethik*, 22 (1978), 60–70.

7. In J. Gremillion, ed., *The Gospel of Peace and Justice: Catholic Social Teaching Since Pope John* (Maryknoll, N.Y.: Orbis Books, 1976), 513–629.

8. Pontifical Commission "Justitia et Pax," *The Church and Human Rights*, Working Paper no. 1 (Vatican City, 1975).

9. N. Goodall, ed., *The Uppsala Report 1968: Official Report of the Fourth Assembly of the World Council of Churches* (Geneva: World Council of Churches, 1968).

2

Christian Faith and Human Rights

Human Rights and the Tasks of the Church and Theology

In many places and cultures throughout the world, the rise of insights into the basic rights and duties of human beings has coincided with the understanding of the humanity of persons. What is involved here is not an exclusively European or Christian idea, although at the time of the Enlightenment human rights, not independent of Christian influence, entered into the processes of constitution making in Europe and North America, and so attained a worldwide political significance. Today, however, it is particularly the peoples of the Third World who through their struggle for freedom and self-determination have impressed upon all human beings and states the urgent necessity of recognizing and realizing fundamental human rights.

The declarations of human rights considered valid today in the United Nations (even though they have not been ratified by all member states) are to be found in the *Universal Declaration of Human Rights* of 1948 and in the *International Covenants on Human Rights* (The International Covenant on Economic, Social, and Cultural Rights; The International Covenant on Civil and Political Rights; The Optional Protocol to the International Covenant on Civil and Political Rights) of 1966. We have to be aware of the fact, however, that on the basis of their various political, economic, and social histories, the nations emphasize and seek to realize different aspects of human rights. For example, under the influence of the misery caused by fascist dictatorships, the North Atlantic states have formulated *individual human rights* over against the state and society. In their struggle against capitalism and class rule, the socialist states have given preeminence to *social human rights*. The nations of the Third World are demanding the *right to economic, social, and political self-determination*. Human rights, therefore, cannot be viewed as abstract ideals but must be looked, at against the background of the suffering and of the present struggles of individuals, nations, and states.

The task of Christian theology is not one of trying to present again what thousands of experts, lawyers, legislators, and diplomats in the United Nations have already accomplished. But neither can Christian theology allow itself to dispense with the discussion of and the struggle for the realization of human rights. On the ground of the creation of man and woman in the image of God, on the ground of the incarnation of God for the reconciliation of the world, and on the ground of the coming of the kingdom of God as the consummation of history, the concern that is entrusted to Christian theology is one for the humanity of persons as well as for their ongoing rights and duties. The specific task of Christian theology in these matters is grounding fundamental human rights in God's right to—that is, his claim upon—human beings, their human dignity, their fellowship, their rule over the earth, and their future. It is the duty of the Christian faith beyond human rights and duties to stand for the dignity of human beings in their life with God and for God.

The church, Christian congregations, and ecumenical organizations have the clear task and duty of identifying, promoting, and realizing human rights. Since they are neither private associations nor statutory authorities yet must exist and work in the public eye, those Christian organizations can be expected to be less influenced by their self-interests and to be better able to enter the struggle for human rights with less prejudice than other institutions. This is why one can expect from them self-criticism as well as criticism of the egoism of the nations, states, classes, and races in which they find themselves; hence one can also expect their witness to a human solidarity with all those who bear the human countenance and, more particularly, their willingness to stand up for those robbed of their fundamental rights and freedoms.

God's Claim upon Human Beings

Christian theology, on the strength of biblical witnesses, is related to God's dealing with people in history. What is at issue here is the liberation and redemption of human beings from their sinful godlessness and their deadly inhumanity, and thus also the realization of their original destiny through having been created in the image of God.

According to the Old Testament, Christian theology reflects the liberation of Israel from slavery in Egypt, the covenant of the liberating God with the liberated community, and the rights and duties of the people of God which are implied in the covenant of freedom. Liberation, covenant, and the claim of God are the basic content of the biblical witness of the Old Testament and indeed they are found in this order. They have decisive directional power for Israel and Christianity in particular, and exemplary significance for all human beings and nations. The human rights to freedom, to community, to dominion, and to the future are inseparable constituents of God's claim upon human beings and the whole creation; they make up the inalienable dignity of human beings living in a covenant relation with God.

According to the New Testament, Christian theology reflects the liberation of human beings from sin, law, and death through the coming, the sacrifice, and the resurrection of Jesus Christ. In the lordship of the crucified Son of man, the vicious circle of evil, "which must bear ever greater evil," is broken through, and the freedom of the children of God begins to appear. Liberation through the vicarious death of Christ, the new covenant in his blood, and the new rights and duties of the fellowship which is composed of slaves and free persons, Jews and Gentiles, men and women (Gal. 3:28) are the basic content of the biblical witness of the New Testament. Because in his coming, his sacrifice, and his resurrection Christ is "the visible image of the invisible God,"

21

human beings in his fellowship become his brothers and sisters and set out on the way toward the realization of their human destiny as the image of God in the world. Herein lies his grace and their dignity.

By reflecting the liberation, the covenant, and the claim of God according to biblical witnesses, Christian theology also discovers the freedom, the covenant, and the rights of human beings today, and therefore brings out the pain caused by their present inward and outward enslavements, as well as the struggle for their liberation from these enslavements, toward a life of dignity, rights, and duties in fellowship with God. In a world which is not yet the kingdom of God, Christians cannot leave any area of life without witness to the divine liberation, the covenant of God, and the dignity of human beings. The biblical witness to liberation, covenant, and God's claim leads to a corresponding Christian practice and theology.

The universal presupposition of the particular history of God's dealing with Israel and with Christianity is found in the reality that the God who liberates and redeems them is the Creator of all human beings and things. Thus in God's liberating and redeeming action the original destiny of human beings is both experienced and fulfilled. In the "image of God" concept, the divine claim upon human beings is expressed. Human rights to life, freedom, community, and self-determination mirror God's claim upon persons, because in all their relationships in life—human beings with each other and creatures with the creation—they are destined to reflect the image of God.

The universal purpose of Israel's and Christianity's particular experience of God is found in the reality that the God who liberates and redeems them is the fulfiller of the history of the world, who will bring his claim upon his creation to realization in his kingdom. Thus, his liberating and redeeming action in history reveals the true future of human beings; the image of God is their real future. In all their relationships in life—human beings with each other and creatures with the creation—they therefore have a right to future. Human rights mirror the claim of the coming God and of his future upon human beings.

God's claim upon human beings was and is experienced in concrete events of the liberation of human beings, in their covenant with God and in the rights and duties inherent in their freedom. Image of God, as destiny, points to God's indivisible claim upon human beings and therefore to their inalienable dignity.

Fundamental Human Rights

By *fundamental* human rights we mean those rights and duties which belong essentially to what it means to be truly human, because without their being fully acknowledged and exercised human beings cannot fulfill their original destiny of having been created in the image of God.

The Image of God Is Human Beings in All Their Relationships in Life. Human beings in the fullness of their lives and in all life's relationships—economic, social, political, and personal—are destined to live "before the face of God," to respond to the Word of God, and responsibly to carry out their task in the world implied in their being created in the image of God. They are persons before God and as such capable of acting on God's behalf and responsible to him. As a consequence of this, a person's rights and duties as a human being are inalienable and indivisible.

Economy, society, and the state have to respect this dignity and responsibility of human beings, for their role as human beings, with rights and duties, comes before any constituting of society and government. Respect for freedom of conscience is the foundation of a free society. Often in monarchical folklore and in political ideologies, the king alone is called the image of God. "The shadow of God is the prince and the shadow of the prince is the people" (*Babylonian Mirror of the Princes*). Only the ruler can function as mediator between the gods and the people. When the Bible calls human beings the image of God, this constitutes a fundamental criticism of the divinization of the rulers and their ideologies of rule. Not the king, but the individual human being alone is mediator between God and the people. Human beings do not exist for the sake of rule; rule, rather, exists for the sake of human beings.

From this follows the democratization in principle of every kind of rule by human beings over others. The rulers and the ruled must be recognizable in like manner and in common as being human. This is possible only when there is an equality under the law for all citizens. A constitution (the covenant) must guarantee the fundamental human rights as basic rights of the citizens. It must bind together those who are ruling and those who are ruled. Only on the basis of equality under the law can expression be given to the common human identity of rulers and ruled alike. The human rights and duties implied in the image-of-God concept are honored in history through the constant, open, and incessant process of democratizing the shaping of the people's political will. The control of the exercise of rule through the separation of powers, the limitation of the mandate to rule to a stipulated period of time, and the extensive self-rule and participation of the people are the historically developed means for honoring the image of God present in human beings.

If human rights are based on God's claim upon human beings and if human freedoms are rooted in liberation by God, then we also have to formulate the fundamental human duties without which those rights and freedoms cannot exist. Freedom and rights by themselves mean virtually nothing. Just as it is crucial to formulate the dignity and the rights of human persons over against the state in order to limit and control power and to cooperate in its exercise, so it is equally important to heed the duties which correspond to these rights and which human beings must exercise for the sake of others. Among these duties we should mention in our present discussion the *right to resistance* and the *duty to resistance* against illegal, illegitimate, and inhuman regimes in favor of the right of the neighbor.

According to the Reformed confessional writings, one is required to obey the authorities "insofar as they do not command that which is contrary to God" (Zwingli, *Zurich Disputation*, 1523, Summatory Articles, No. 38). "Therefore all their laws shall be in harmony with the divine will . . ." (39). "But if they are unfaithful and transgress the laws of Christ they may be deposed in the name of God" (42). As a consequence of the divine covenant of freedom, human beings are called "to save the lives of innocents, to repress tyrannie, to defend the oppressed" (*Scottish Confession*, 1560, Article 14).

The rights which secure the freedom of the individual can only be observed if they are bound up with the corresponding duties of liberating those from whom these rights are withheld. Christian love honors the rights of the neighbor.

The Image of God Is Human Beings Together with Others. Only in human fellowship with other people is the human person truly an image of God (Gen. 1:28). The history of freedom in Europe and North America was one-sided in emphasizing the individual rights of the human person over against economic, social, and political organizations of rule. It is the error of liberalism to over-look the social side of freedom, and it is the failure of individual-ism to overlook the social consciousness that must correspond to the human personality. It is not against his or her fellow human beings nor apart from them but only in human fellowship with them and for them that the individual can correspond to his or her destiny as created in the image of God.

In fellowship before God and in covenant with others, the hu-man being is capable of acting for God and being fully responsible to God. As a consequence of this, the social rights and duties of the human community are just as inalienable and indivisible as persons' individual rights and duties. Human beings have to heed the dignity and the responsibility of community in economy, soci-ety, and state, just as the latter has to heed those of the former. It does not follow from the democratization of the rule of human beings over others that every human being is his or her own absolute ruler. Just as according to Gen. 1:27 the image of God appears in the fellowship between husband and wife, so it is also represented in larger social contexts only through human fellow-ship. Thus the rights of human beings to life, freedom, and self-determination always arise together with the human community's claim upon people. In principle there is *no* priority of individual rights over social rights, just as conversely there is no priority of social rights over individual rights. Both stand in a genetic context of reciprocal conditioning just as historically the processes of the socialization and the individualization of people mutually condition each other.

The rights of persons can only be developed in a just society, and a just society can only be developed on the ground of the rights of the person. The freedom of the individual can only be constituted in a free society, and a free society can only be constituted on the ground of individual freedom. Human liberation is liberation for community and human community is community in freedom.

Individual societies and states, in their social rights and duties, are responsible not only to the people who live in them but also to humanity. Human rights thus also entail humanity's claim upon individual societies and people. If particular political and social communities are bound through their constitutions to the human rights of their citizens, they must also be bound, on the other hand, to the rights of humanity. Collective egoism threatens human rights just as much as individual egoism. Thus, individual communities and states are only legitimized by human rights when they respect not only the human rights of their own citizens, but also to the same degree those of other nations and peoples. Human right is indivisible; it is no privilege. Therefore, national foreign policy can only be legitimized as the world's domestic policy. International solidarity in overcoming the horror of starvation and the threat of world military crises has, therefore, because of the rights of humanity, a precedence over loyalty to one's own people, to one's own class, race, or nation. Individual communities and states have human duties in the face of the rights of the whole of humanity to life, freedom, and community. Therefore, human rights point to a universal community in which alone they can be realized.

Being Created in the Image of God Is the Basis of the Right of Human Beings to Rule over the Earth and of Their Right to Community with the Non-Human Creation. In Gen. 1:28ff. the creation of human beings as the image of God is followed by the blessing of God and the human calling to be fruitful and rule over the nonhuman creation. Human rule over the earth is to correspond to the will and command of the Creator who loves his creation. Human beings are to "till and keep" the earth (Gen. 2:15) and to rejoice in it. Only where human dominion over the earth corresponds to the Creator's lordship over the world do human beings fulfill their creation in the image of God. Plundering, exploitation, and the destruction of nature contradict their right and dignity. Therefore, human dominion over the earth includes a sense of community with the earth. Human rule is only then made legitimate when it is exercised in cooperation and community with the environment and leads to life-giving symbiosis between human society and the natural environment. The right of human beings to rule over the nonhuman creation must therefore be balanced by their respecting the "rights" of the nonhuman creation.

If the right to the earth is given to human beings, it follows that each and every human being has the basic economic right to a just share in life, nourishment, work, shelter, and personal possessions. The concentration of the basic necessities of life and the means of production in the hands of a few should be seen as a distortion and perversion of the image of God in human beings. It is unworthy of human beings and contradicts God's claim upon them. The widespread withholding of basic economic rights, the impoverishing of whole peoples and population groups, and worldwide starvation caused by political and economic imperialism in our divided and strife-torn world are a desecration of the image of God in people and of God's claim upon each and every person. Without the realization of the fundamental economic rights of human beings to life, nourishment, work, and shelter, neither their individual nor their social rights can be realized.

If along with the right of human beings to the earth *"rights" of the earth over against human beings* are recognized, then basic ecological duties are also bound up with these basic economic rights. It is not possible to increase basic economic rights at will simply by responding to increased demands, because economic growth is determined by ecological limits. The human struggle for survival and world domination cannot be carried out at the expense of nature, since in that case ecological death would anyway prepare the way for the end of human life altogether. Economic human rights should therefore be brought into line with the basic cosmic conditions for the survival of humanity in its natural environment. These rights can no longer be realized through uncontrolled economic growth, but only through the growth of economic justice within the limits of growth. Economic justice in the provision and distribution of food, natural resources, and the industrial means of production will have to be directed toward the survival and the common life of human beings and nations. This is the only way of attaining ecological stability in mutual survival as well as in a common life alongside the nonhuman creation. Today economic and ecological justice mutually condition each other and thus can only be realized together.

Being Created in the Image of God Is the Basis of the Right of Human Beings to Their Future and Their Responsibility for Those Who Come after Them. Human beings in all their relationships in life—with each other and in community with the nonhuman creation—have, as the image of God, a right to self-determination and responsibility for their future. Their true future lies in the fulfillment of their being destined to the glory of their fellowship with God, with other human beings, and with the whole creation. In human history in which the kingdom of glory is not yet realized, human beings correspond to this dignity for which they were created through their openness for this future and through their responsibility for the present in the face of this future. By virtue of their "citizenship in the kingdom of God," through which they gain their dignity, human beings have a right to their true future as well as corresponding duties in the shaping of life in the present.

People can only make use of their right to this future and their responsibility to the present if they attain the freedom of *responsibility* and the right to *self-determination*. Self-determination and responsibility to the present in the face of the future relate (1) to human beings in all their relationships in life, (2) to human beings in community with others, and (3) to human beings in community with the nonhuman creation. This is an important dimension in the basic individual, social, economic, and ecological human rights and duties. There are no human rights in the present without the right to self-determination and one's own responsibility in the face of the future, for people live personally, collectively, economically, and ecologically in time and history. Their eternal and their temporal futures therefore also have claims upon them. The political recognition and pursuit of human rights ultimately gain their significance in this perspective of the future. Human beings become free and affirm their rights and duties as their true and eternal future gains power over them in hope and conditions their present.

Thus, in accord with this future, they will stand up for the right to a temporal future and the right to life of those who come after them. They will struggle not only for justice in the world of their own generation but also for the support and preservation of justice in generations that will follow. There exists not only a personal and a collective egoism, but also an *egoism of the generations*. Thus people should not exploit their present at the expense of the future, just as there is no obligation to sacrifice their present to the future. Rather, they should work for a just balance between the opportunities of life and freedom in the present and in the future generations. In a time of overpopulation and of "limits of growth," this temporal perspective of human rights assumes particular significance. Economic politics; population politics; health politics; and, under certain circumstances, genetic politics, should be directed toward the human rights of the present and future generations.

The Justification and Renewal of Human Beings

Human rights are only effective insofar as people are truly human and act humanly. Their inhumanity becomes manifest in the violations and abuse of human rights. This is why, behind the practical question as to how human rights may be realized on earth, there are the more profound questions as to where people can experience their true humanity and how they can overcome their actual inhumanity.

Ever since the *Universal Declaration of Human Rights* in 1948, political violations of human rights have been brought to the awareness of world public opinion. This has brought to light how serious and widespread are the everyday violations of the fundamental rights of human beings through power politics and unjust authority, through hate and fratricide. The growing use of torture under dictatorships is a terrifying indication of the fact that the *Declaration of Human Rights* and its public acceptance have not in themselves created a new humanity among the nations. Nevertheless, the *Declaration of Human Rights* sharpens people's consciences and renders any inhumanity illegitimate.

Moreover, since the discussion on the *International Covenants* of 1966, it has become clear that human rights are not only violated but also abused. They are abused whenever they are used ideologically to justify private interests over against the rights of other human beings. They are abused whenever they are divided up and it is pretended that only part of them stand for human rights in their totality. It is then that we see the birth of individual egoism, national arrogance, humanity's imperialism over nature, and the absolutism of the present generation over future generations. The increasing ideological abuse of human rights is one further indication that declarations and ratifications alone do not create true humanity among human beings. Nevertheless, insight into the indivisible totality of human rights sharpens people's consciences and sense of responsibility for each other.

Christian theology uses the word *sin* to describe people's inhumanity as it is made manifest in continued violations and abuse of human rights. According to the testimony of the Bible, human beings have failed to come up to their original destiny to live as God's likeness on earth, and they still fail to do so today. They wanted to "be like God" and thereby lost their true humanness (Genesis 3; Romans 5). Enmity therefore characterizes humanity's relationship to nature (Genesis 3), and with Cain's murder of his brother begins the history of a humanity that does not want to be "its brother's keeper" (Genesis 4). And so people's sin perverts their relationships with God, their Creator; with their fellow humans, their neighbors; and with nature, their home. God to them becomes a judge, fellow human beings become their enemies, and they become estranged from nature. Today fear and aggression dominate a divided and hostile humanity which is on the way totally to destroy itself and the earth. Human rights can only be realized when and insofar as the justification of unjust human beings and the renewal of their humanness take place.

The Christian faith recognizes and proclaims that God through Jesus Christ justifies unjust human beings and renews them to their true humanness. Through the incarnation of Christ, God restores to human beings who want to "be like God" their true humanity that they had abandoned. Through the death of Christ, God takes the judgment of people's sin on himself and reconciles them to himself (2 Cor. 5:19). Through the raising of Christ from the dead, God makes real his claim upon people in that he justifies them (Rom. 4:25). Through the outpouring of his Spirit on all flesh (Acts 2), God renews his likeness on earth, unites a divided humanity, and liberates his creation from the shadow of evil. In the coming of his kingdom, God will ultimately glorify his right, justify human beings, and transfigure creation.

God's claim upon human beings in this world of sin and inhumanity is revealed to Christians through the gospel of Christ (Rom. 1:16–17). Because the divine right of grace is proclaimed to all people through this gospel, the God-given dignity of each and every person is proclaimed in conjunction with it. But where this human dignity is revealed, fundamental human rights are also made to come in force. Their realization is made possible and becomes therefore an undeniable commitment.

On the strength of the gospel, human rights in a hostile and inhuman world are first and foremost made real through the ministry of reconciliation (2 Cor. 5:18ff.) Faith separates the human person from inhuman sin. Love accepts the person and forgives the sin. Hope perceives the human future of the person and opens up new life. In this way—through faith, love, and hope—humanity, once betrayed and lost, is restored to the people. Through the service of reconciliation, human dignity and right are restored in this inhuman world. Wherever people's dignity is recognized and their right restored, there this service of reconciliation takes place. Reconciliation is nothing less than justifying justice; it is the power of the new creation in this twisted world.

For the sake of reconciliation one can therefore forego one's own right. For the sake of the neighbor's right, one can suffer up to the point of giving one's life. Selflessness and sacrifice in the "service of reconciliation" of the world with God are always also selflessness and sacrifice in the service devoted to the true humanity of people. Christians have the divine calling to bring the *right of reconciliation* to bear on the worldwide struggle for privileges and power, in which they are witnesses to the future and agents of hope. For with the right to reconciliation there begins here and now a process in which the present unrecognizable world changes into a world that will be seen to be a human world loved by God. The experience of reconciliation turns enemies into friends. Working at reconciliation opens up the future of life to people who are threatened by death. Sacrifices in the service of reconciliation are the seeds of hope. Without reconciliation, the humanization of situations as they are is impossible. Without their humanization, reconciliation remains ineffective. Reconciliation and change belong together, and together they bring about humanness in this world.

It is the task of Christians, in the existing world conflicts in which they live, to proclaim the gospel of justification, to live the liberating faith, to exercise the ministry of reconciliation, and to give in their congregations a demonstration of a reconciled humanity in the fellowship of men and women, Jews and Gentiles, slaves and free persons (Gal. 3:28). It is especially when Christians fulfill these specifically Christian tasks that they serve the realization of the humanity of all people. By proclaiming God's justifying justice they proclaim the dignity of human beings. By practicing the right of grace they practice basic human rights. The Christian faith therefore does not excuse us from the struggle for the recognition and realization of human rights, but leads us into this very struggle. The community which calls Jesus "Son of man" suffers under the ongoing inhumanity and dehumanization of human beings, and in its prayers turns this suffering into a painful awareness.

Priorities and Balance in the Struggle
for Human Rights

Because human beings as individuals, in community, and in humanity are meant to reflect the image of God, all human rights are bound up with and related to one another. One can neither curtail them, separate them from each other, nor differentiate among them. Furthermore, all human rights are bound up with specific human duties. Rights and duties cannot be separated from each other; privileges should not grow out of rights nor empty demands out of duties.

But in human history, people and nations, responding to the needs in which they find themselves, always set priorities. When the economic need stands in the foreground, they seek first to realize basic economic rights. Where political oppression is reigning, they seek first to realize political rights. Every progress in one area of life, however, causes the structure of life to get out of balance. The one-sided, uncontrolled, and uncoordinated economic growth in some nations has pushed the political, social, and personal balance of human beings in these societies to the edge of destruction. The hegemony of the developed industrial nations has kept other nations in conditions of underdevelopment and has made them dependent. The sudden development and securing of personal freedoms and rights can weaken social rights and duties, just as conversely the one-sided extension of social rights can lead to the weakening of personal rights. Thus partial progress in one area of life must be constantly accompanied by the redressing of the balance of human rights in other areas. Progress without balance is destructive just as balance without progress degenerates. The real history of the recognition and realization of human rights is accomplished in the constant conflict between progress and balance, a conflict which cannot be solved within time.

Whoever honors human beings as the image of God must acknowledge all human rights in the same degree and therefore view them in their indissoluble relationship to each other. Whoever heeds the inalienable dignity of human beings must, in the conflict

33

between progress and balance, look to the unity of human rights, the human rights of people in all their relationships of life, and the rights of the whole human race. It follows that in the one-sided progress in the development of human rights in one area, human rights in another area of life should never be fundamentally suspended. To bring this partial progress in harmony with human rights then becomes an irrevocable demand, because otherwise the balance of the whole structure of life cannot be won back, nor can human dignity be wholly honored.

In the conflict of human history, people always live with a disturbed balance in their human rights. Their human dignity appears in a somewhat distorted form; therefore it is necessary, in order to realize the totality of human rights, to develop strategies which eliminate the inequalities inevitably resulting from established priorities. In countries which purchase their sudden economic progress at the expense of political rights and individual freedom, one must press for the realization of political and individual human rights. In countries which secure the personal freedoms of their citizens at the expense of the social rights of the community, these collective rights and duties must be promoted. In societies which have established social rights at the expense of individual rights, individual human rights are to be promoted. In dependent and underdeveloped countries, the rights of independence and self-determination have priority. The acknowledgment of the inalienable dignity of human beings and the insight into the indivisible unity of their rights and duties can be regarded as regulative ideas and in various situations and societies can establish priorities and produce balance.

On the basis of their various histories, individuals, peoples, and nations have given particular emphasis to differing aspects of human rights. They must establish their priorities in different ways in order to escape from inhuman conditions, from want, violence, and dependence; and so their concerns for human rights vary. However, the concept of the indivisibility and thus the unity of human rights should act as a pointer to the future of a universal established community of all people and nations. The right to different concerns must be integrated into the higher right of the just *balance of concerns* because, without such balance, humanity will not survive its conflicts.

Accordingly, the following can be expected from Christianity, churches, congregations, and ecumenical organizations:

1. In the struggle for human rights and political priorities they will represent the unassailable *dignity of human beings* and thus also the indivisible *unity of their human rights and duties*. Both are constituted through the claim of the one God upon persons in all of their relationships of life.

2. In various situations of people and nations, they will press for the *restoration of those particular human rights* which through one-sided progress and established priorities have become neglected, weakened, or repressed.

3. They will overcome their own egoism in order to *overcome the egoism* of individual, social, and human rights over against nature and the egoism of the present generation over against the coming generations, in order to serve the humanity of each and every person in the interest of God their Creator and Redeemer.

4. Through public proclamation and education they will sharpen the duties of the individual which are inexorably bound up with the *rights* of human beings with regard to their God-given dignity, to other people, to nature, and to the future.

Christianity understands itself as witness to the triune God who liberates human beings from inward and outward inhumanity, who allows them to live in his covenant, and who leads them to the glory of his kingdom. Christians therefore stand up for the dignity of human beings out of which emerges their rights and duties. For the sake of God they will stand up with all means at their disposal, acting as well as suffering, for the dignity of human beings and their rights as the image of God. For their service to the humanity of persons they need the right to religious freedom, the right to form a community, and the right to public speech and action.

3

The Right to Meaningful Work

The Right to Work and the Meaning of Work

The *right to work* is not a demand for just any kind of work but for humane work, work that is meaningful for human beings. But is work meaningful at all for human beings?

"Do you believe it would be ideal to live without having to work?" Thus read a question in a national survey in Germany. Answering yes in 1962 were 18 percent; in 1975, 25 percent; and in 1976, 30 percent.[1] That is not surprising.

For thousands of years in premodern society, work was regarded only as toil and burden and therefore felt to be meaningless.[2] Meaningful life existed only outside of work, for meaningful life existed only in freedom. Work did not liberate; it enslaved.

It was modern Europeans—that is, the inhabitants of the middle-class world of industrial society, of urban civilization—for whom work first moved consciously into the center of life. Their life is dependent on and arranged around work. Their self-images, social recognition, worth, and therewith, plainly, even their essence depend on their work and are measured by the results of their work. For the middle-class, urban, industrial society is no longer a society of class and family but essentially a society of production. "The human being is what he or she produces," and he or she is worth as much as he or she produces or can afford on the basis of his or her production. It is therefore understandable

37

that for many of our contemporaries the meaning of their lives depends on the possibility of work and on the quality of their work. It is also understandable that for many people life becomes meaningless when they are unemployed or must do work to which they cannot relate.

Does it make sense, however, to seek the meaning of life in work? Can work have such power? Does such an expectation not lead to excessive demands on work and to torment for human beings?

We seem to fall into an irresolvable contradiction. On the one hand people in modern society are dependent on work; therefore, since the beginning of this society, it has been necessary to lift up the demand for recognition and maintenance of the human right to work. On the other hand, however, the existing, essential, and paying jobs in this society are not always ones that can guarantee people a meaningful life. How does the right to work relate to the *meaning of life,* and how is the meaning of life connected with the right to work?

Here we will look at the concept of *meaning* broadly and develop it in three dimensions: (1) What is the significance of work for the working person? (2) What is the significance of work for the human community? (3) What is the significance of work for life in general, for the meaning of the whole?

We will go into the ethical significance of work and treat it as follows: (1) the work of God, (2) work as vocation, (3) work as enterprise, (4) work as achievement, and (5) work as participation in the history of the kingdom of God.

The Work of God

In the ancient world, *work* meant the toil and burden of maintaining and reproducing life. Life had to be wrested from an unordered, hostile environment. Yet this struggle itself was not true life but only its precondition. In his or her work a person was still enslaved; only the result of a person's work could be called freedom. Work could thus be seen as the process of mediation between the human being and world, between civilization and nature—necessary, to be sure, but not in itself meaningful. Out of this process came only the economic support of human life, namely, the cycles of acquisition and consumption, birth and death. Freedom, life, and human worth were found only beyond this unavoidable process of material change. Therefore, it was not fitting for the free citizen himself to work. The lower cycle of life was delegated to slaves, serfs, and women. Work had no permanence; work was no accomplishment, for it was not a virtuous activity. Work did not reflect the beauty and the *logos* of the gods. Permanence, deeds of virtue, beauty, and meaning for life were created only by free citizens in the formation of the *polis*, of public life, and of civilization.[3]

In Greek civilization there were no actual gods related to work except for Hephaestos and other patrons of the crafts. Homer's true heaven of the gods was the work-free world of eternity. Therefore, the true human being corresponding to the gods was defined by *logos, nomos,* and *polis* and not by *erga* and *pragmata.*

> Activities fall into those that are appropriate to the free man and those that are not fitting for him. Obviously, therefore, among the useful occupations, he can pursue only those that do not turn the one who pursues them into a worker (*banausos*) and injure his bodily and spiritual human dignity . . . that is, those that do not make the free man unfit for the dignified enjoyment of existence and for the various occupations appropriate to his virtue. . . . It is impossible for one who leads the life of a *banausos* or daily wage earner to practice deeds of virtue.[4]

This separation of virtue and work manifestly reflects a slave-holding society. In it, not only is cheap labor exploited for the sake of profit. But rather, work itself is understood as enslavement: "To work means to be a slave to necessity."[5] Because people are subjected by nature to the necessary satisfaction of life's needs, they can only become free if they subjugate others and force them to achieve this maintenance of life. The disenfranchised class of slaves and women is, therefore, simply a reflection of the idea of the meaninglessness of work. Work makes one unfree, and whoever is unfree is condemned to work. Work defiles, and whoever is defiled has to work.

These few remarks on the concept of work in ancient slave-holding society should indicate how prevalent even today are the separation of work from meaning, the desire to be free from work, and the delegation of vitally necessary and life-sustaining work to other people or to machines. We have spoken not of the distant past, but of a present development. Whether it is desirable or not is yet to be decided. A person's conception of work always stands in close relationship to his or her understanding of the gods or of the meaning of his or her life. Even if the gods themselves disappear from sight, the hope and meaning placed in them remain definitive.

The first thing that biblical traditions say about work concerns the work of God. Certainly, Yahweh is no subordinated worker-god. Rather, he is the slave-freeing God, as the first commandment states, "who led you out of the house of bondage." Therefore, he is the Creator who calls the nonexistent into being. Everything visible and invisible is "the work of his hands." To be sure, the exclusive theological use of the word *barah* sets the creative work of God apart from all possible human works, but in and through their work *in* the world human beings can and should correspond to the creative activity of God, from which the world emerged:

> Six days you shall labor and do all your work . . . for in six days the Lord made heaven and earth, the sea, and all that is in them. . . . The seventh day is a sabbath to the Lord your God . . . [he] rested the seventh day (Exod. 20:9–11).

At the beginning of creation there was no work-free age as in Greek mythology. On the contrary, Gen. 2:15 states: "God took the man and put him in the garden of Eden to till it and keep it." Not work itself, but work after the fall is regarded as work cursed by toil, pain, and uselessness. Therefore the deliverance of human beings from sin actually cannot lead also to deliverance *from* work, but only to a transformation of their work from curse to blessing.

We can characterize the Old Testament conception of work as follows: Here work is neither cursed as slavery nor sanctified as service to God. Work and virtue, work and freedom, work and meaning are neither theoretically nor practically separated, as in the slave-holding society. They are rather brought into correspondence. The commandment to work and rest is based on its correspondence with the creating and resting of the Lord. In work and rest human beings, in their way, take part in the creative world process and in the joy of the Creator. In contrast to the ancient dichotomies, this makes work itself meaningful.[6]

Work is thus meaningful not because it alone provides the meaning of life, but precisely because it is limited by the goal of rest and joy in existence. The Sabbath does not simply interrupt work. Rather, work is understood and defined through the Sabbath. There is more to this ordered relationship of work days and holidays than just mutual boundaries. Work day and Sabbath lie also on the same temporal level. They concern the same people. They are not divided between human beings and gods or between slave and free. Therefore, they also overflow into each other and affect each other.

When people through their work earn their livelihood and produce their life, when they glorify God and partake of his rest on the Sabbath, then they also present themselves before God. Consequently, life has not only a producing value in work, but also a presenting value in the joy of existence. Producing and presenting overflow into each other, for in each production we also present ourselves as we are and as we understand ourselves. Theologically this means that people work and rest "in the presence of God." Anthropologically it means that work contains, for human beings, not only production value but also existence value. Therefore, humane work cannot consist only in acting for purpose and usefulness. It must also encompass freedom for self-presentation and thus playfulness. This is true also for the social process as a whole: We plan and produce history; but we also, therefore and thereby, present ourselves and attempt to reveal and know ourselves. In the seriousness of work also belongs, in a human sense, the relaxed joy of existence: "Let it be!"[7]

In the biblical traditions there is another group of specifically theological assertions about work. In them work is not related to the effortless creation of God, but appears in the connection between "pain and work." Here we are dealing with the "work of redemption." Creation out of nothing is a relatively easy task compared to the redemption of sinners. On the blotting out of the sins of God's people, Isa. 43:24f. says:

> You have burdened me with your sins, you have wearied me with your iniquities. I, I am He who blots out your transgressions for my own sake, and I will not remember your sins.

And the chosen one, who according to Isaiah 53 brings the salvation of God to the wicked, is designated as worker, "servant of God," *ebed Yahweh*. His soul has "worked," and he "carries" iniquities like a porter. What is important for a theology of work is not that Jesus was a carpenter or a carpenter's son—no matter what is held by modern Catholic Josephology—but rather that his passion story is patterned after and recounted according to the model of the "servant of God" in Deutero-Isaiah, that according to Philippians 2 his way was that of servanthood, and that, according to the Gospel of John, the crucified one says of his "work," "It is finished," and thus in the divine servanthood his universal lordship takes place for all. The point here is God's action in his suffering, in his renunciation, in his voluntary servanthood and self-surrender. God creates salvation by suffering the torments of prisoners. He frees them by his renunciation. He wins them by his servanthood.

In the designation of this redemption as the "pain and work of God," the word *work* gains a new meaning. It is filled to the highest degree with theological content. *Work* becomes the embodiment of the doctrine of salvation. In this process, of course, work and freedom are again separated and divided into two different subjects: through God's work people are freed from sin. And thereby the ordering of slave-holding society is turned upside down: God is our slave—we his free people!

But, when it is demanded of "anyone," as Paul says, that he or she should "be of the same mind as Christ" (Phil. 2:5), then this theologically rich understanding of "pain and work," which is filled with the aim of salvation and the goal of freedom, is redirected to human beings. This twofold hermeneutical process in the biblical tradition has completely transformed the concept of work in Christianity. Anyone who inquires about the work ethos of the Bible runs up against the cultural history of past societies if he or she only investigates the statements on human work. One will not arrive at a theology of work in this manner. Nor will one arrive at a biblical doctrine of work by means of the concordance method.[8] The transference of the human concept of work to God and especially to his redeeming activity, then the redirection of the concept to human beings who are supposed to correspond to God, has had an enormous effect and still has today. The dialectic of servanthood and lordship in the Christ hymn in Philippians 2 became, through Hegel and Marx, the basic model for the modern philosophy of work.

Let us return one last time to the biblical traditions: in correspondence to the servanthood of Jesus, Paul conceived of his own apostolic activity as work. The proclamation of the gospel is a necessity (*ananke*), which he cannot escape (1 Cor. 9:16f.). Therefore in this service he becomes a "*servant* of Jesus Christ" (Rom. 1:1). The apostolic work carries all the marks of the servanthood of Christ. In more than ten places he calls missionary and congregational work a *kópos*. That is an expression that designates the heaviest, most unpleasant work of slaves. In 2 Cor. 11:23–28, he holds up to his opponents the fact that he has "worked more" than all others and counts as his "work"—labors, imprisonment, beatings, mortal danger, persecution, slander, hunger, thirst, cold, nakedness, and constant concern about the congregation, which he describes as follows in Gal. 4:11: "I am afraid I have labored over you in vain." The apostles are "fellow workers for the kingdom of God" (Col. 4:11). Through them people become members of the kingdom and friends of God.

What Paul says about general working activity for the sake of maintaining life actually falls into the category of a "parergon," as Barth called it.[9] Yet all of those works are placed in the service of Christ's lordship and are supposed to serve as participation in the kingdom of God. Such is the import of those generally held formulas that all work takes place "for the sake of the Lord" (1

Thess. 2:12; 4:9–11; 1 Cor. 7:17), "for the sake of Christ" (2 Thess. 3:6; Acts 20:35; Col. 3:17; *et passim*). What Paul says directly about such work differs little from the Stoic-Cynic diatribe. But if he understands apostolic activities as "work" and "servanthood" in correspondence to and participation in the mission and self-dedication of Jesus Christ for the kingdom of God and the freedom of humanity, then this extended meaning of work also sheds new light on the original concept. All work in the world is thereby placed on the level of Philippians 2 and filled with the hope of the kingdom of God.

Through faith work is not just relativized or exorcized. Rather, it receives through faith a messianic meaning. That work "is not in vain in the Lord" is substantiated by the resurrection hope in 1 Cor. 15:58.

What happens in work is nothing less than co-renunciation with Christ and hope for co-regnancy with him. In this way work "for the sake of the Lord" receives a meaning that reaches beyond every success of the work. If work can be used in following the self-renouncing Christ, then it also promises participation in the resurrection and in his kingdom. In this way earthly work receives the stimulus of a hope that moves people constantly to invest more and give more of themselves than is necessary and therefore also to expect from work more than the earthly results justify. The added value of the messianic hope also results in added effort, self-denial, and self-giving. It is especially this excess of expectation that unbalanced the traditional work ethos in static forms of society and opened it up to the newness of the future.

In the biblical traditions we find three unforgettable changes in the concept of work:

1. The creating God finds his counterpart in the working human being. The God who rejoices in his work finds his counterpart in the human joy in being and joy of self-presentation.

2. Through pain, work, and self-renunciation God accomplishes the deliverance of imprisoned humanity. Work and servanthood become the embodiment of God's liberating and delivering action. Through servanthood God comes to his lordship in the world.

3. The reapplication of this theological meaning of work to human beings induces them, through work and self-giving, to participate in the lordship of Christ in the world and thereby to become co-workers in God's kingdom, which completes creation and renews heaven and earth.

Work as Vocation

The ancient separation of virtue and work, of meaning and work, and their assignment to different social classes was, of course, overcome in principle by the Christian monastic orders with their motto *"Ora et labora."* Nonetheless, the *vita contemplativa* took precedence. Mary had still chosen the better part. Prepared by the popular movement of mysticism and the Brothers of the Common Life, it was the Reformation that first overcame that ancient separation. The rediscovery of the "general priesthood of all believers" (Leipzig Disputation, 1519) overcame in principle the splitting of the church into priests and laity: every believer is *vocatus, conversus,* and *religiosus.* "All Christians truly belong to the priestly class, and there is no difference among them" ("To the Christian Nobility," 1520). In the *Kirchenpostille* of 1522, for the first time, Luther coined for this the term *vocation (Beruf),* which includes the call both to faith and to work in one's occupation.

With this bold identification of the call to be a Christian with the particular place of the call, the whole weight of the religious significance of life falls on this one spot. Luther considered this perception the third main point of the Reformation. In the Schmalkaldic Articles he enumerated them: "Through God's grace our churches are prepared and enlightened (1) by the pure Word of God and (2) by the proper use of the sacraments and (3) by recognition of all kinds of occupations (*vocationes*) and proper works" (BS 411).[10] This shows that the Reformation was understood not only as reformation of the church but, at the same time, as reformation of the world, that is, as reform of the working conditions of Christians. In its works worldwide Christianity follows its divine call and fills the whole world with the charismata of the new creation; reformation is the beginning of the eschatological *reformatio mundi.*

Every honest vocation is service to God: That is why one maid, who goes out as ordered and according to her duty sweeps the yard and carries out the manure, goes directly to heaven on the straight road, while another, who goes to St. James or to church but leaves her duty and work undone, goes straight to hell (*Weimar Ausgabe* [*WA*], 10, 1, 309).

Then a poor servant girl could seriously have joy in her heart and say: Now, I cook, I make the bed, I sweep the house. Who ordered me to do it? My lord and my lady ordered me to do it. Who gave them such power over me? God did. Indeed, it must be true that I don't serve them alone, but also God in heaven. How can I be more blessed?! It is just as if I wanted to cook for God in heaven (*WA* 53, 471).

That is also the doctrine of work of the Protestant hymnal, the influence of which cannot be overestimated:

Gib, dass ich tu mit Fleiss,	Grant that I may work hard
was mir zu tun gebühret,	to do what I am supposed to
Wozu mich Dein Befehl	do, for I am led in my
in meinem Stande führet	position by your command.
Und streck nun aus mein Hand,	And (let me) now stretch out
greif an mein Werk mit Freuden,	my hand and grasp with joy
dazu mich Gott bescheiden	my work, which God has
in mein Beruf und Stand.	assigned to me in my
Paul Gerhardt	vocation and position.

Certainly, these verses do not give expression to a justification by works, but rather to middle-class integrity in vocation and position.

According to this interpretation, the call through the gospel meets us where we are, namely, in our position in society, and turns our position into our vocation. All meanings, characteristics, and hope of the divine call to community with Christ thereby fall on the work appropriate to one's position: self-denial, loyalty, fulfillment of duty, love of neighbor, honesty, blamelessness, acceptance of suffering for Christ's sake, and a good conscience for eternity. The Prussian-Kantian, civil-servant ethos comes from this understanding of work as vocation.

Nevertheless, this doctrine of work remains unclear:

1. God calls people directly through the gospel and at the same time indirectly through the occupational structure of society,

through the law. Because it is the same God, there can be no dissonance or contradiction here. But how is one to decide in case of conflict?

2. One must find a common theme for these two voices. If one follows Article 16 of the Augsburg Confession, then one may not dissolve political and economic structures but must preserve them as *ordinationes Dei* in order to practice love within them. One must be obedient to one's political, familial, and economic authorities "insofar as this can be done without sin." Unfortunately, this proviso was often overlooked.

The history of Lutheranism as well as Lutheran ethics shows that Luther's bold identification of vocation with the call led again and again to the integration of the call into vocation and vocation into occupation, and thus to the consecration of the *vocational-occupational structure:* "Vocation began to gain the upper hand over the call; the Word of God on the right (gospel) was absorbed by the Word of God of the left (law)."[11] This is exactly what led to enormous torment of conscience in conflict situations, as the "20th of July 1944" demonstrates. Even apart from that kind of spectacular event, one looks in vain in the appropriate areas of Lutheran ethics for viewpoints on a change of vocation. Since the call comes once and lasts a lifetime, it is obviously supposed to be the same with vocation. A change of vocation smells of disloyalty, autocracy, and fanaticism.

Even this understanding of work is not just a matter of the past, but is desired in the present German scene: all workers become employees, and all employees become civil servants, so that in the end the entire population is composed of civil servants; a total civil-servant nation?

Today this vocational ethos is still possible only in a very limited way:

1. On theological grounds the *call* to be a Christian happens but once; it is irrevocable, immutable, and directed toward the hope of the coming glory. It admits one into the community of Christ and leads to the path of discipleship. *Vocations,* on the other hand, are historical, changeable, limited by time, and directed toward neighbor and society. Vocations are undertaken, shaped, and changed according to the call. "The worldly voca-

tion receives new legitimacy from the gospel only to the extent that it is practiced in discipleship to Christ."[12] Vocations are not confining, crippling prisons for the mandate of Christian hope but possibilities and opportunities for hope in action.

2. The Lutheran vocational ethos was only possible in a class society in which each person already at birth had a fixed position from which duties and expectations could be derived. But even in such a class society this ethos was not able to include everyone because not everyone was blessed with a position. The "class of the classless" was always left out of the vocational ethos. The civil servants and the clergy were most easily able to live this vocational ethos.

3. In a working society of interchangeable work places and jobs, that vocational ethos disappears. At its best this society gives people a multiplicity of opportunities for change. At its worst it forces people constantly to relearn. It requires flexibility, adaptability, willingness to change, and imagination, but not loyalty to vocation and employer. Vocational work in a fixed occupation gave a person outward security and inner peace. Persons knew who they were and how they were regarded: "Mr. Pastor" and "the tailor's wife." The mobility of the modern worker society robs a person of this external security. It requires superior inner identity and freedom of the individual vis-à-vis his or her work. Otherwise it threatens a person with an accommodation that tears him or her apart.

Work as Enterprise

This step toward sovereign individuality was first accomplished by the Calvinist Christians and the allegedly fanatical groups on the so-called left wing of the Reformation in the early industrialized countries of Western Europe.[13] Here work was conceived as enterprise, not as vocation. While for Luther vocation resulted from the harmony of call and occupation, here one heard only the call through the gospel and experienced the inner voice of the Holy Spirit. No one perceived the voice of God in the world and in society. Therefore the world became raw material for fulfillment of duty, for the pioneer spirit, and for enterprising investments. Success alone justifies work. Successful work, however, proves the proficiency of human beings, and proficiency justifies the existence of human beings. For continental Lutheranism a person's occupation was his or her destiny, his or her home. One had to resign oneself to it. In Western European Calvinism, as Max Weber has clearly shown, work in a vocation became something in which Christians had to demonstrate their faith, election, and proficiency. Therefore, the boundaries of class and guild were no longer respected: "Make what you can—save what you can—give what you can," John Wesley advised Christians. The effect was the unlimited earning, amassing, and investing of capital that we call capitalism. From this follows, on the one hand, the individualization and isolation of people, who find themselves essentially in a competitive struggle with everyone else.[14] "Survival of the fittest" is their only hope. On the other hand, the result is the objectification of the natural environment into raw material to be exploited for minerals and energy. Ecological catastrophe is the price of that power struggle.

How does this development affect the meaning of work? Max Weber pointed to the new discipline of life. If persons cannot rely on divine order in society anymore, then they must take the regulation of their lives into their own hands. Through constant self-examination they gain control over themselves. Through self-control they become lords of their lives. Work is the preferred means of getting oneself into shape. A job change, self-chosen or decided by one's employer, is the best way to remain free, flexible, young, and available. Anyone who wants to settle down somewhere is out of the running. Members of this accelerated, industrial society must feel "like strangers in a strange land," explained Alvin Toffler.[15] In order to remain unreservedly at the disposal of their firms and corporations, the career model of mid- and upper-level management requires a maximum of inner adaptability and outer mobility and reduction to a minimum of close ties to family and friends. Somewhat more positive in tone is the description of "enterprising work" by the Walter Raymond Foundation:

> Diligence, initiative, perseverance, willingness to take a risk, a feel for economic opportunities, saving, investment of profit in the enterprise mark the entrepreneur in the industrial age.

Can we recognize here those whom Max Weber described as "self-conscious saints," whom we find in the steel-hard Puritan businessmen of that heroic age of capitalism and, in isolated examples, even in the present?

1. The Puritan ethos has in no wise disappeared. It is still alive in those denominations and sects that encourage social climbing. People get ahead through hard work and willingness to accept any employment, through frugality and abstinence from smoking, drinking, and pleasures and then find themselves visibly blessed by success. In Latin America the Pentecostal and Baptist congregations, through the inner spiritual certainty and strict morals that they foster, promote the ascent out of the slums and into the middle class.

2. The Puritan ethos, however, has long since been transformed into the "spirit of capitalism," has been secularized in it, and through it has brought us to the edge of self-destruction and environmental disaster. Therefore, the Puritan ethos is less and less enlightening and no longer fills people's work with meaning.

3. Reduction of the meaning of work to the working subject and contempt for the social as well as the religious dimension of meaningful experience contradict every biblical tradition and theological perspective. Work is not exhausted by its subjective meaning any more than the call is absorbed in one's vocation in society.

Work as Achievement

One pervasive expectation of the modern era is that work must be creative work if it is to have meaning for human beings. Humane work is understood as individual, creative action: individual because through it a particular person brings his or her being to expression; creative because this expression is unexchangeable and unrepeatable. In creative work persons not only create something according to their own ideas; in it and with it they also create their own selves. They realize their being. They come out of themselves and to themselves. Creative work is self-realization, achievement of individual identity: I am, because I work. I am what I make of myself. Thereby work becomes a mirror that tells persons who they really are. It becomes the revelation of their hidden inner selves.[16]

In this connection, Hegel's philosophy can be regarded as the first "philosophy of work."[17] It has a theological point: according to the biblical witness, human beings through their work correspond to the creative God. According to Thomas Aquinas, a person through working resembles the ground of the world, which is understood as *actus purissimus*. For Hegel, the spirit is "pure activity," "absolute restlessness." He conceives the active, restless spirit not in itself but in its history, which he calls the self-realization of the absolute spirit. How does the absolute spirit realize itself? Through its self-renunciation for its other, through its self-surrender to its opposite, and through the reappropriation of itself. World history is the process in which the absolute spirit works, and this process follows the dialectic of renunciation and appropriation, of the negation of itself and the negation of this negation. In this dialectical process the spirit produces itself. It becomes for itself what it in itself is.

It must be noted that this god, who is understood as *actus purus* or pure activity, knows no Sabbath. In this respect, he is a heathen god. This divine process is exactly what human work must emulate. The dialectic of renunciation and appropriation is repeated in human work—one gains one's identity by going out of oneself and coming to oneself: "The working consciousness comes thereby to the perception of independent existence as its self." If self-realization of a human being happens in human work, then it happens through self-renunciation. That has nothing to do yet with "alienation." One attains identity through renunciation and lordship through servanthood. The *analogia Christi* is unmistakable here: the Christ hymn of Philippians 2 is the archetype of the modern philosophy of work, even if that process is accomplished only by a subject without help from an exalting God.

Therefore, it was logical for Karl Marx to reduce Hegel's dialectic of work to the subject "human being." For humanity the highest being is the human being. For Marx that means: "What the [individuals] are, coincides with their production, both with what they produce as well as with how they produce."[18] Nowhere else does one find the *mirror* that shows who he or she is. Industry alone is "the open book of the human powers of being." If work is understood as such a mirror of being, wage earners can see themselves only as alienated, torn apart, exploited, and deceived. If they take the working world as the mirror of their being, then it shows them not their being, but their nonbeing; not riches, but poverty. For work is not a creative renunciation, but a self-destructive alienation. Their work, which they themselves do not determine, and the product, which they themselves do not possess, shows workers only caricatures of themselves, their deformation, their dehumanization. Life and work in the alienated world of capitalism are destroyed beyond recognition.

Out of this critique comes the revolutionary imperative "to overthrow all conditions in which a person is a humiliated, enslaved, forsaken, and despicable being."[19] As the capitalist society constantly alienates the working person, so the communist, that is, "all-human" society must produce the all-human person as its constant reality. In it a person can acquire "his all-rounded being in an all-rounded way." A person will be able to recognize himself or herself in the "mirror" of his or her work, so that the "total loss" of humanity is followed by the "total regaining of humanity."

Work as achievement of human essence places a person's self-knowledge in his or her work. The concept of work as the *mirror of human nature* remains, especially where Marx is thinking of a transformation of constantly alienating work into pure spontaneity. Then out of "pain and work" comes the harmony of "renunciation and appropriation of human nature."

Work, understood as achievement of the human essence, leads to a specific promise: Work is to be an achievement that provides a creative, unified, and humane community. If it does not fulfill this expectation, then it produces alienation, dehumanization, and an inhumane society.

Work as achievement requires total effort and complete self-giving. This can be required, however, only if and as long as the utopian hope insists on full earnings and complete self-realization. If the hope is lost, then the effort can no longer be justified and mobilized.

The crucial anthropological question at this point concerns the mirror for the perception of human nature. Can work be this mirror? Can every production become a self-portrait? Does the true mirror, in which we know ourselves, perhaps lie elsewhere—in any case, not in our own works, which we transcend? Can a person ever "be absorbed in his or her work?"[20]

Work as Participation in God's History

If, in conclusion, we attempt to summarize the various viewpoints from which work has been judged meaningful, then it is certainly not with the claim of a comprehensive, generally binding understanding of work. We have seen, rather, that various groups and classes in society have each developed their own work ethos. Nonetheless there are many common threads. Otherwise one would have to place limits on the expression *work*.

The same applies to the meaning of work. It also diverges according to group and class and does not let itself be easily generalized on the basis of any particular value. That becomes especially clear if one raises the question of the relationship between the meaning of work and the meaning of life. Work has a quite varied significance for the meaning of life. It ranges from total identification—"His work is his life"—to total separation—"If you work and don't shirk, you're a jerk." Yet there are common threads concerning the meaning and the humanity of work, even if only the commonality of disagreement among the divergent viewpoints. In summary, we return to the three dimensions mentioned at the beginning:

1. *What is the significance of work for the working person?*

In the relationship between work and subject, it is a matter of life-support and self-realization.

A person works because he or she must earn a living. This is meaningful to the extent that living is meaningful for him or her. But since that is not the only possibility—because one can also live without working—the meaning of life cannot rest merely in the supporting of life. Nevertheless work instills in a person feelings of independence and ability and thus self-consciousness. Every unemployed person knows that. Certainly, one can also affirm existence in other ways. Nonetheless, the "active affirmation of existence" (Barth) gives a person his or her own worth.

No one *has* to justify himself through work. No one *has* to demonstrate her right to existence through work! No one *has* to realize himself through work. Were that true, then the unemployed would have no rights and the handicapped no reality. Only if this dehumanizing inward or outward compulsion to work is removed can there be a right to work for every person according to his or her abilities. Whoever has to work because he or she is compelled to needs no right to work. The right to work presupposes freedom. Because of freedom, however, the right to work becomes indispensable. It is especially when not all of life has to be work, that work has a significance for a person that goes beyond work. It is, therefore, inhuman to increase the efficiency of human work according to the Taylor system to the point where all that remains are those manipulations that even an ape can accomplish. Is it not also inhuman to want to make human work technologically superfluous? The value of work for the working person will be won through humanization of the work place, through communal work, through the collective and individual decisions of the workers concerning their work—or else it will be lost altogether.

If work alone is not the mirror of humanity, it must for that very reason be fashioned in such a way that a person can affirm it in its essence, because in it he or she experiences an affirmation of his or her own essence. The expression *self-realization* is too strong, because it threatens the young, the old, the handicapped, and the unemployed with nonexistence. Work is experienced as humane when it provides latitude for individual formation and thereby allows possibilities for self-expression.

This is no idealistic carry-over of an artist's work to that of a wage earner. When all regularly recurring work processes can basically be carried out by computer, the development and proliferation of free, responsible, "creative" activities will be not only a possibility, but also an urgent necessity. In businesses, spontaneous horizontal relationships are more sensible than hierarchical chains of command. In the end, confidence is better than control.

2. *What is the significance of work for the community?*

Because most jobs today, especially in service industries and social services, require cooperation, work also aids in the socialization of the individual. Through work a person enters the social process, participates in it actively, and is recognized by other people and by society as a whole. Through work a person gains companions, colleagues, and friends. Unemployment threatens a person with the loss of this community and with social death. This dimension seems to become more and more important. Destruction of the working community through conditions of power and dependence *dehumanizes* work.

"Work is the foundation for the production of goods," says the *DTV-Lexikon* (Munich). "Work is purposeful, conscious activity for the creation of useful products," says *Meyer's Kleines Lexikon* (VEB Leipzig). That sounds like "total-German" unity. One does not recognize socialism or capitalism in these definitions because they are from the early industrial period. But work is defined too narrowly if one speaks only of vocation, hired labor, enterprising and thus productive work, and the like. Other areas of work from which a society actually lives remain unconsidered and are pushed aside or forgotten. Work is wrongly defined if one means only productive work and forgets reproductive work. Finally, work is also understood in only a limited way if jobs in service industries and social services are not designated as *work*. The restriction of the concept of work to productive work was perhaps correct in the early industrial period. In the wake of automation in production, it is misleading.

For a long time, work was understood only as a means to an end. The object was to produce the greatest number of goods with the least amount of work. Therefore, the quality of work was only negatively restricted by work protection rules. This *product-oriented* concept of work is one-sided. It robs work itself of its human significance. In a certain sense, work is always an end in itself. There is a human meaning in work, even apart from the production of goods. People sense it in the feelings of satisfaction that work can give them. In order to understand this human meaning that lies in work itself, we need a *work-oriented* concept of work. Only with it can we comprehend what work suitable for people is. Certainly one concept of work cannot be set against another. On the contrary they can complement each other and provide mutual protection against one-sidedness.

We recommend, therefore, that work be understood in a comprehensive sense as active participation in the social process. That includes housework as well as service industries and social services. Every citizen, male or female, has a right to participate in the social process according to his or her strengths and capabilities. On the other hand, a logical consequence of this participation is the demand for proper payment for *all* work through which people participate in the social process.[21]

3. *What is the significance of work for the meaning of life?*

It is not inconsequential whether or not the work of people and the working process of society have meaning for the whole. Statements on the theology of work in antiquity, in the biblical traditions, and in modern Protestantism have shown that. Considering the basic ideas, we can say the following in summary:

In his or her work a person corresponds to the creating God.

In his or her work a person participates in God's self-emptying for the purpose of liberating humanity.

In his or her work, even if not in it alone, a person realizes his or her call to freedom.

In his or her work and through it, a person is on the promised road to the kingdom of freedom and human worth.

If one seeks a concept that includes the significance of work for the person and for society, then the expression "work in the kingdom of God" is near at hand. In the nineteenth century, of course, it was reserved for missions and diaconal ministry. But it is also able to show the eschatological meaning of all work and of society itself in its historical dealings with the natural world. The world is not finished. Through their work people take part in the destruction or the preservation of the world. They serve not only with the creating God; they also work together with the redeeming God. A rare but outstanding example of what is meant here is "the kingdom of God in industry," the phrase of Gustav Werner in Reutlingen.[22] Gustav Werner wanted to prepare the way for the kingdom of God not only diaconally and charitably, like Bodelschwingh in Bethel, but also constructively and in the middle of the industrial world. Thus, for that purpose, he founded cooperative factories.

In the promise of the kingdom of God which renews heaven and earth, there comes against the growing destructive potential of human societies an urgent call for resistance against death, passion for life, and community within history. It seems sensible to me to consider this perspective in dealing with questions of vocation, work, wages, and the like. For in the end this is "the one thing that is necessary": "Seek first the kingdom of God, and all these things will be added unto you."

NOTES

1. M. and S. Greiffenhagen, "Das schwierige Vaterland," *Der Spiegel,* Sept. 1979: 54ff.

2. The Middle High German *arebeit,* ancestor of the modern German *Arbeit,* "work," meant trouble, toil, need. Calvin used the French word *travail,* "work," to designate vexation and suffering.

3. Hannah Arendt, *The Human Condition* (Garden City, N.Y.: Doubleday-Anchor, 1959).

4. Aristotle *Politics* 1276bff.

5. Arendt, *Human Condition.*

6. W. H. Schmidt, *Die Schöpfungsgeschichte der Priesterschrift,* 2d ed. (Neukirchen, 1976), 51ff.

7. J. Moltmann, *Theology of Play,* trans. Reinhard Ulrich (New York: Harper & Row, 1972).

8. Cf. the attempts of Alan Richardson, *The Biblical Doctrine of Work* (London: SCM Press, 1952); W. Bienart, *Die Arbeit nach der Lehre der Bibel* (Stuttgart: Evangelischer Verlagswerk, 1954); M. D. Chenu, *The Theology of Work: An Exploration,* trans. L. Soiron (Chicago: Regnery, 1966).

9. Karl Barth, *Church Dogmatics,* 3/4, §55, "The Active Life."

10. K. Holl, *Die Geschichte des Wortes Beruf,* SAB (1924), 29–57; G. Wingren, *Luthers Lehre vom Beruf* (Göttingen, 1952).

11. Barth, "The Active Life."

12. Dietrich Bonhoeffer, *The Cost of Discipleship,* trans. R. H. Fuller (New York: Macmillan, 1959).

13. Max Weber, *The Protestant Ethic and the Spirit of Capitalism,* trans. Talcott Parsons (New York: Charles Scribner's Sons, 1958).

14. This is shown by C. B. MacPherson, *The Political Theory of Possessive Individualism* (New York: Oxford University Press, 1962).

15. Alvin Toffler, *Future Shock* (New York: Random House, 1970), 187. Toffler calls the new human type of super- or post-industrial society "the Modular Man."

16. Cf. Th. Litt, *Das Bildungsideal der deutschen Klassik und die moderne Arbeitswelt* (Bonn, 1955).

17. For this see Roger Garaudy, *Gott ist tot. Eine Studie über Hegel* (Berlin, 1965), esp. 64ff.

18. K. Marx, *Frühschriften,* ed. S. Landshut (Stuttgart, 1953), 347. Obviously, modern industrial work has fundamentally dissociated itself from the traditional, middle-class work ethos. Although the positive anti-type of the "total," "all-rounded and deep-thinking person" itself still belongs to the middle-class educational ideal, nevertheless the negative critique that follows from it expresses best the attitude of factory workers toward their work: "that the work is external to the worker, that is, does not belong to his essence; that in his work he feels himself not affirmed but negated, not happy but unhappy; that he develops no free physical and spiritual energy, but wrecks his body and ruins his spirit. Hence, the worker feels close to himself only outside of work and in his work estranged from himself. He feels at home, when he is not working, and when he is working, he is not at home."

19. Ibid., 216.

20. For this criticism see Jürgen Moltmann, *Man: Christian Anthropology in the Conflicts of the Present,* trans. John Sturdy (Philadelphia: Fortress Press, 1974).

21. Cf. A. Hüfner, *Recht auf Arbeit. Ein Lesebuch* (Verlag Atelier im Bauernhaus, Fischerhude, 1978); U. Achten, *Recht auf Arbeit—eine politische Herausforderung* (Neuwied, 1978); *Technologie und Politik. aktuell Magazin* 6: Die Zukunft der Arbeit 1, rororo aktuell, 4184, 1977.

22. P. Krauss, *Gustav Werner. Werk und Persönlichkeit* (Reutlingen, 1959).

PART II

RESPONSIBILITY FOR THE WORLD AND CHRISTIAN DISCIPLESHIP

4

Luther's Doctrine of the Two Kingdoms and Its Use Today

In its four-hundred-year tradition Protestantism has developed two different theological conceptions with whose help the Christian faith can clarify its historical situation and its political commission. These two conceptions are the Lutheran doctrine of the two kingdoms and the Reformed doctrine of "the lordship of Christ."

These two doctrines also characterize the attitude of the German Protestant churches toward the state during the church struggle under the National Socialist dictatorship. On the basis of the two kingdoms doctrine, the Lutheran state churches (*Landeskirchen*) maintained a "neutral" position as documented in the Ansbach Decree of 1935. On the basis of the doctrine of the lordship of Christ, which determines the whole of life, the Confessing Church took up the position of resistance, as can be seen in the Barmen Theological Declaration of 1934. Furthermore, the very strong differences in postwar Germany—to this day—over questions of politics and social ethics find their basis in the difference between these two conceptions.

Whether it has to do with questions of nuclear armament, the recognition of the Oder-Neisse border, the contracts of the social-liberal government with the Eastern Bloc, the ordering of private property, the question of abortion, the World Council of Churches' Program to Combat Racism, or aid for development, division will appear along lines associated with these two doctrines again and again. On the one side, the side of the two kingdoms doctrine, these questions are defined as nontheological and are pushed away into the "kingdom of the world" to be dealt with only from the point of view of political reason and expedience; the other side, however, seeks to place such fundamental political decisions within the meaning of obedient discipleship under the lordship of Christ.[1]

The obstinacy with which both of these concepts are maintained shows that it is not simply two different models of theological ethics which are at stake here; rather, the roots of the difference lie in the understanding of the gospel and of faith itself. In order that these concepts of theological ethics be understood, it is therefore necessary to clarify the underlying understanding of the gospel contained within them. For without examination and clarification of the differing basic dogmatic positions there can be no change in the political orientation of the church and of faith.

As regards the relations of faith and politics in Protestantism, we have to do in the first instance not with a problem of ethics but with the basic problem of theology itself. As long as a Christian does not know what true Christian faith is, he or she cannot relate in a reflective way to political questions. As long as the church does not know what the true church is, it cannot change its relationship to the state. This of course is overlooked today when out of an inner uncertainty in faith one plunges into political engagement in order to find a more certain standpoint. Without new certainty in Christian faith and action, however, there is no political relevance in the struggle for the liberation of the oppressed and for justice in the world.

The newer "political theology" is developing within the ecumene, on the Catholic and Protestant side in common, a third concept. It has begun with the revision of fundamental theological decisions in order to overcome the differences in the political orientations we have mentioned.

The following essays will introduce the most important aspects of these three theological concepts. They cannot, of course, be any more than an introduction, for each of these theologies is a world of its own, each having its own extensive library of exposition and polemic. In order to make an overview and a comparison possible, I will focus on the following topics in the treatment of each theological concept:

1. The basic theological positions.
2. The interpretation of history which follows therefrom.
3. The relationship of theory and praxis.

Although Lutherans constantly appeal to Luther's two kingdoms doctrine[2] and its use in Lutheran tradition, there is no one uniform doctrine, but many. Even in Luther's writings and certainly in the Lutheran tradition there are many very different conceptions of the two kingdoms. In Lutheran confessional documents (the so-called Book of Concord) there is no strictly formulated two kingdoms doctrine. In the relevant Protestant dictionaries two quite different articles on this doctrine often appear, both written by Lutherans.[3] The Lutheran lawyer Johannes Heckel spoke of the "garden of errors of the two kingdoms doctrine" and did not mean by that simply the immeasurable expanse of literature, but also the unclarity of the subject matter itself.[4]

A look at actual practice merely increases the confusion. Whereas some Lutherans in West Germany support politically conservative powers with the help of the two kingdoms theory, Lutherans in East Germany live in and work with a state socialism by appealing to the same theory.[5] While German Lutherans used this theory to justify favorable neutrality in the Third Reich, the Norwegian Bishop Berggrav used it to provide the rationale for his resistance against the Nazi tyranny.

Bishops and church leaders are not the only ones who seek to clarify the relationship to the state by means of the two kingdoms doctrine. Politicians and governments also do it. The priests must not preach "politically," threatens the Polish government, which has forbidden the union Solidarity. It is often claimed in dictatorships such as South Korea, the Philippines, South Africa, and Argentina that "freedom of religion" is a guarantee, but those who draw nonconformist consequences from their religion are branded as enemies of the state. One might generalize and say that every dictatorship practices its own form of the two kingdoms doctrine over against the church. The question is, Who erects the border between the two kingdoms, the church or the government? Who is the subject of the distinction between the two kingdoms?

The two kingdoms doctrine does not seem to offer a particularly bright beam for guiding those pressed by political and ethical questions. How then should we account for its strength and obvious attraction?

The Basic Theological Position: Apocalyptic Eschatology; History Is the Apocalyptic Conflict Between God and the Devil

Luther was an Augustinian monk. His early writings show him as an independent representative of the late medieval Augustinian renaissance. When he speaks of the two kingdoms in this early period he takes up the Augustinian tradition and means by this struggle of the *civitas Dei* (city of God) against the *civitas diaboli* (city of the devil), a conflict which rules world history until the end.[6] The expressions *civitas* (city) and *regnum* (kingdom) can be interchanged, but it is always the conflict between Jerusalem and Babylon, between Cain and Abel, good and evil, God and the devil which is meant when he speaks of the two kingdoms.[7]

Just as this conflict between the two kingdoms dominates world history, it also dominates the personal life of the Christian as the continual conflict of the spirit against the flesh, justice against sin, life against death, faith against unfaith. This struggle of faith which leads to mortification of oneself and vivification in the spirit will find its end only when the power of sin is conquered in the resurrection of the body and death is swallowed up in the victory of life.

In principle, then, the battle between God and the devil in world history and in personal life is understood eschatologically. In fact, to be more precise, this eschatology is an apocalyptic eschatology which speaks of a real but as yet unrealized future and also of a still outstanding struggle at the end.

Whether the young Luther speaks of world history, church

history, or personal history, he always thinks in terms of the antithesis between *civitas Dei* and *civitas terrena, regnum Christi* and *regnum diaboli, corpus Christi* and *corpus mali,* faith and sin, spirit and flesh. But it is never a matter of a dualism of two different levels or two separated domains which could coexist with each other peacefully; rather, a conflict, contradiction, and struggle in the *one* creation and the *same* human being. Insofar as his two kingdoms doctrine means the eschatological struggle between the *regnum Dei* and the *regnum diaboli,* it is a doctrine of struggle and its distinctions are of a polemical nature.

But what is the cause of this conflict? Seen historically, Luther takes up in his two kingdoms doctrine Augustine's *De civitate Dei,* but with it also the early church apocalyptic of Tyconius and behind that the apocalyptic view of history of ancient Judaism as the prophet Daniel had formulated it. Not only the history of Israel but also world history is determined by the conflict of two world aeons. This perishing aeon of the injustice of the bestial world rulers will be overcome by the new, coming, and eternal aeon of God's righteousness. Therefore, in history the pagan peoples struggle against God's people of Israel and the godless sinners against the righteous who trust God. The whole of history is a slaughterfield of the coming eschatological struggle of the end time. The life of the individual believer is also such a field. The true reason for this struggle lies in the election of Israel as the people of God in the midst of the godless nations and in the election of the righteous who keep the law of God in the midst of the lawless masses of human beings.

Understood from a Christian perspective, the cause of the apocalyptic conflict of the end time lies in the coming of Christ, the coming of the gospel and of faith. Through the proclamation of the gospel this conflict is inflamed, and through faith it is recognized. For the sake of the saving kingdom of Christ two kingdoms must be spoken of, for in salvation corruption is simultaneously revealed, and with the coming of Christ comes also the antichrist. The preaching of the gospel occasions the decision of faith, the simultaneous separation of the faithful from the unfaithful, Christ from antichrist.

The decision of faith for God is always a decision against the devil. Thus this decision provokes an eschatological conflict in the world and in the life of every single person. Because God and faithful human beings correspond to each other, human beings in faith contradict the godless world, and the world contradicts them and leads them into temptation, trials, and suffering.

But the two kingdoms theory which speaks of this conflict between the reign of God and the reign of the devil would not be Christian if it were only to transmit this apocalyptic world view. Only when this conflict results from the coming of Christ and from the coming of faith, and Christ and faith are themselves the initiators of the eschatological conflict, does this two kingdoms theory have a Christian and not a political foundation. For the sake of the kingdom of Christ, therefore, the conflict between the two kingdoms must be spoken of.[8]

Only when this is clear can two kingdoms for the sake of the reign of the world (*regnum mundi*) also be spoken of. At this point the doctrine of the two kingdoms begins to become ambivalent: In the "fall" the world raised itself in rebellion against God, but it is still God's creation. The devil has become "lord of this world," but the world is still the creation of God. As a result, the world finds itself in self-contradiction: It is godless, but God in his faithfulness will not let it go. By removing itself from its origin in God, it has fallen into destruction out of its own guilt. That it still remains, however, shows that God patiently and gracefully preserves it in spite of its turning away. Equally, every human being is also a creature and a sinner at the same time, and is both of them totally.

The liberating kingdom of Christ is set in contradiction against the kingdom of the devil, but it wants to save the world from this self-contradiction to make it again into God's good creation. The reign of Christ, therefore, is at one and the same time *against* "this world" as the kingdom of the devil, and *for* the world as God's creation corresponding to Christ. Because in everything worldly, both elements—that which contradicts God and that which is creature of God—are inextricably bound up with each other, the kingdom of Christ obtains a twofold relationship to the *regnum mundi*. Gerhard Ebeling has, with Karl Barth, fittingly characterized this relationship as "*contradiction* and *correspondence*." The contradictory relationship is in view when the *regnum mundi* as *regnum diaboli* or as *civitas Babylonica* stands over against the *regnum Christi*. The relationship of correspondence is in view when the *regnum mundi* as creative, earthly, and temporal world points to the coming eternal kingdom of God.[9]

Believing human beings relate to themselves in the same way. As sinners they contradict God; as justified they correspond to the Creator. As long as history lasts they are constantly and simultaneously both and are therefore in struggle with themselves. For this reason they pray: "Lord, I believe, help my unbelief."

It is, I believe, completely wrong to want to divide the world as it is or human beings as they are into two parts—one which contradicts God and the other which corresponds to God. The two kingdoms doctrine does not intend that, although its adherents have often made just this of it. Rather, it is more concerned with two total aspects of the world and human beings—that is to say, two different perspectives: self-contradiction of God and self-correspondence to God. The total world and the whole person is meant every time. Contradiction and correspondence remain in conflict until the ultimate present of the kingdom of God.

The Dual Doctrine of the Two Kingdoms

If the two kingdoms doctrine has its theological origin in apocalyptic eschatology, then its ambivalence has the same source as that of apocalyptic: the *regnum mundi* is, on the one hand, "this perishing aeon of injustice" or the *regnum diaboli* but, on the other hand, God is also Lord of this world insofar as he is the Creator. The *regnum mundi* is therefore also *regnum terrena* (kingdom of the earth). U. Duchrow has thus proposed that it would be better to speak of a "three kingdom doctrine."[10]

Already in Luther himself we find the twofold distinction. The first concerns the great opposition between *regnum Dei* and *regnum diaboli,* between spirit and flesh, the true believers in God and the servants of the devil. The second concerns the correspondence of the creature to the Creator: the creation is temporal, God is eternal; the creation is historical, the kingdom of God is future; the creation is full of signs and shadows of the eternal truth, the glory of God is perfect. These distinctions do not contain anything that is contradictory to God. In the struggle against the *regnum diaboli* the kingdom of Christ takes these creaturely correspondences in politics, economics, the household, art, and science into its service without identifying with them. Luther could therefore occasionally say: *"Omnes ordinationes creatae sunt Dei larvae, allegoriae, quibus rhetorice suam theologiam: sol alls Christum in sich fassen."*[11]

Within the larger distinction between the *regnum Dei* and *regnum diaboli* which rules the whole of world history, the two kingdoms doctrine also makes a second distinction between the saving kingdom of Christ and the preserving kingdom of the world. For the delimitation and dissolution of the devil's power God has instituted two different regiments: the spiritual regiment and the worldly regiment.

Within this second distinction both kingdoms, the "kingdom of the world" and the "kingdom of Christ," are directed against the "kingdom of the devil," but in different ways. Each of these two kingdoms has its own justice: the one the *justitia civilis,* and the other the *justitia Dei.* In the worldly kingdom law, good works, reason, the punishing sword, and rewards for good deeds are valid. In the spiritual kingdom of Christ only grace, justification, and faith are valid. In the worldly kingdom the sword rules, in the spiritual kingdom the Word rules. In the spiritual kingdom God provides eternal salvation. In the worldly kingdom human beings must care for the temporal welfare.

Luther worked out this distinction between regiments in his well-known treatise, "Temporal Authority: To What Extent Should it be Obeyed" (1523). I pick up the flow of the argument in order to make clear the other fundamental perspective of the two kingdoms doctrine. Luther begins with the great distinction:

> Here we must divide Adam's children and all people into two parts: the first is those who belong to the kingdom of God, the rest belong to the kingdom of the world. Those who belong to the

kingdom of God are all those who are true believers in and under Christ. For Christ is King and Lord in the Kingdom of God . . . and he also came that he might begin the kingdom of God and establish it in the world. . . . The people need no worldly sword nor rights, and if all the world were true Christians, that is, true believers, then there would be no prince, king, sword, nor rights needed or used. . . . To the kingdom of the world or under the law, however, belong all who are not Christian. For while few believe and the least conduct themselves according to the Christian manner, of not resisting evil and not doing evil, for those outside the Christian condition and the kingdom of God, God has created another regiment and has placed it under the sword. . . . For if that were not so because, to be sure, all the world is evil and in every thousand there is scarcely one true Christian, each would devour the other. God has therefore ordained two regiments—the spiritual, made up of Christians and the pious people through the Holy Spirit under Christ; and the worldly regiment which restrains the non-Christians and wicked ones so that they must maintain order and be peaceful without their thanks.[12]

Luther then distinguishes and demarcates the regiments, each with respect to the other:

If anyone attempted to rule the world by the gospel and to abolish all temporal law and sword on the plea that all are baptized and Christian, and that, according to the gospel, there shall be among them no law or sword—or need for either—, pray tell me, friend, what would he be doing? He would be loosing the ropes and chains from the savage wild beasts and letting them bite and mangle everyone, meanwhile insisting that they were harmless, tame, and gentle creatures; but I would have the proof in my wounds. Just so would the wicked under the name of Christian abuse evangelical freedom, carry on their rascality, and insist that they were Christians subject neither to law nor sword, as some are already raving and ranting.

On the other hand, Luther holds that:

Where temporal government or law alone prevails, there sheer hypocrisy is inevitable, even though the commandments be God's very own. For without the Holy Spirit in the heart no one becomes truly righteous, no matter how fine the works he does. On the other hand, where the spiritual government alone prevails over land and people, there wickedness is given free rein and the door is open for all manner of rascality, for the world as a whole cannot receive or comprehend it.

According to Luther, both regiments mutually limit and complement each other. In the worldly regiment law and power serve to bring external order and earthly peace. In the spiritual regiment the Word of God serves to engender faith.

This distinction which Luther draws between the two is thoroughly polemical; in the matter of faith there may be neither laws nor coercion: "Faith is a free work to which no one can compel the other." In the realm of faith, therefore, civil pressure and political oppression must not be used. Even heretics may only be overcome by means of the Word of God and may not be politically persecuted. In the matter of faith it holds that "You must obey God more than human beings." Wherever an authority exercises religious coercion, he must be resisted. The ruler may not interfere with the kingdom of God nor with the spiritual regiment. On the other hand, the spiritual regiment may not interfere with the worldly regiment, for one cannot rule the world with the gospel. Politics is to be executed according to reason and expediency.

Luther often also distinguishes between the two regiments anthropologically. The worldly regiment may not extend further than over the body, goods, and the external parts of the earth. The spiritual regiment extends over the soul and the inner person. More recent interpretations say: The worldly regiment concerns the world relationships of human beings, the spiritual regiment their relationships with God. Luther's distinction according to which both regiments mutually limit and complement each other appears to be the description of ideal conditions, but it was in fact critically directed toward his religious and political situation. Politics is constantly carried out by means of religion. This seduces and corrupts the soul. Religion is constantly practiced by means of politics. That corrupts worldly order and peace.

Luther's two kingdoms doctrine is in its truth a critical-polemical separation between God and Caesar. It permits neither a Caesaro-papalism nor a clerical theocracy. It intended to teach that the world and politics may not be deified, nor may they be religiously administered. One should give to Caesar what belongs to Caesar—no more and no less—and give to God that which is

God's. One should turn the self-deified world into the world, and let God be God. One should deal rationally with the world, with the law, and with force. The world is not and it never will become the kingdom of God; rather it is a good earthly order against evil chaos. One should deal spiritually—which means with faith—with God and his gospel. The gospel does not create a new world but saves people through faith.

Christian Person and World Person

As illuminating as the great and small distinctions of the two kingdoms doctrine may be, when considered with regard to the Sermon on the Mount and the political life of the Christian, it has severe difficulties. Does the Christian serve two lords? Is the Christian a citizen of two kingdoms at the same time? Where are Christians to find a place to stand? On the law of the worldly regiment or on the gospel of the spiritual regiment?

Here Luther makes a corresponding distinction between faith, which justifies before God without the works of the law, and works, which are to be done for the sake of the neighbor alone. When the person is justified before God by faith alone, then works fall out of this justified relationship to God. Liberated from the impossible task of earning access to heaven by way of works, these works now stand totally and exclusively in the service of the neighbor.

In the distinction between faith and works we find again the distinctions which were operative in the two kingdoms theory. In faith the human being is a Christian person; in works, a world person. This is again a critical-polemical distinction: Whoever confuses faith and works will do justice to neither God nor the neighbor. Before God only faith helps; before the neighbor only good works help.[13]

But what are these good works for the neighbor aimed at? The Augsburg Confession says in Article 16:

> The gospel teaches an eternal righteousness of the heart, but it does not destroy the state or the family. On the contrary, it especially requires their preservation as ordinances of God and the exercise of love in these ordinances.

The gospel does not create new orders in the world but rather demands the preservation of the present orders, respecting them as "God's ordinances." Love is to be exercised within them. By ordinance here is meant the state, the economy, and the family. In these ordinances faith becomes effective through love.

The question, however, is, According to which guidelines should love be effective politically, economically, and in the family? According to those of the law or of Christ? Indeed, at the end of Article 16 the Augsburg Confession says that one should obey the authorities and their laws in all these three areas of life, but then adds, "so that it may be done without sin."

Accordingly, Christian love in the worldly regiment stands under the law, by which is meant the law of God, the Ten Commandments, and the natural law as well as the positive laws and decrees of the law books. The limitation upon such laws is that they should not force a person to sin, but this is mentioned without being more exactly formulated. It appears that God has set Christians within his two regiments, so that the Christian as Christ person and world person is a citizen of two kingdoms, of the gospel and of the law. In the spiritual regiment God rules through Christ and faith. In the worldly regiment God rules through the law without Christ.

The impression of a dualism reasonably ensues and has led Lutheran theologians again and again to conform to unjust structures of the state and economy because the criterion for justice in the kingdom of the world was missing. This view of the two kingdoms doctrine only arises, however, if one takes the distinction of both regiments out of the world-historical drama of the battle between the reign of God and the reign of evil and deals with it in isolation on its own. The more both regiments are seen in their common struggle against the kingdom of the devil, the closer they come together and so the clearer their common features become. As Melanchthon says in Article 4/189 of the Apology of the Augsburg Confession: "Because of faith [good works] are nevertheless holy and divine works, sacrifices, and the reign of Christ, whereby he shows his rule before the world. For in these works he sanctifies hearts and suppresses the devil." Through the good works of the faithful in the worldly regiment, the kingdom of Christ reveals itself over against the power of the devil.

According to this view, Christian love in the various circumstances of political, economic, and family life corresponds to the guiding principle of Christ. Even through politics, business, and family life the Christian becomes God's co-worker and a witness to the kingdom of Christ against the kingdom of the devil. Christians will act appropriately and rationally in these various dimensions, but their deeds will be motivated by faith and will be directed toward the salvation of the world. The various areas of life provide the place of Christian action but not the law of these actions. The Christian acts in the relationships of the world but does not act under their compulsion.[14]

Evaluation and Criticism

Summary. We attempt here, cautiously, a diagram of Luther's dual two kingdoms doctrine:

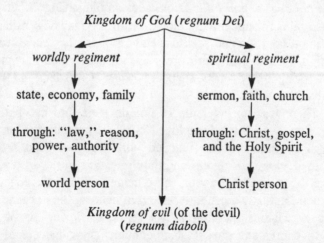

Kingdom of God (*regnum Dei*)

worldly regiment   *spiritual regiment*

state, economy, family   sermon, faith, church

through: "law," reason,   through: Christ, gospel,
power, authority   and the Holy Spirit

world person   Christ person

Kingdom of evil (of the devil)
(*regnum diaboli*)

This scheme makes two different perspectives possible:

1. If we look from the spiritual to the worldly regiment, we see the distinctions: here the Spirit, there force; here faith, there works; here gospel, there law.

2. If we look from the kingdom of God to the kingdom of the

devil, then the spiritual and the worldly regiments come closer together: God fights the power of the devil through both regiments; here with Word and faith, there with order, peace, and law.

3. If we only look at the differences between both regiments then the Christian stands in the paradox of having to be a citizen of two different kingdoms, here required to be obedient to the gospel of the Sermon on the Mount and there required to be obedient to the law and authority of the state. But if we see both regiments in God's battle against the devil, then the Christian, on the basis of faith in God, will do the good works of love against the devilish seed of hate in all worldly places. The worldly orders will thus become places in creation which all "contain Christ in themselves."

The real strife over the correct interpretation of Luther's two kingdoms doctrine has to do with these two perspectives and their ordering.

Misuses, Abusus non tollit usum, goes an old saying. When the misuse gains the upper hand, however, then it may be sensible to suspend a doctrine and seek orientation in another place. I will mention, without systematic order, the misuses which have made the two kingdoms doctrine suspect for many Christians and theologians.

1. There was an inversion of this doctrine into its opposite when it was no longer employed critically-polemically for the sake of disentangling an entangled world but was made instead into an ideology which affirmed the Protestant world. Instead of aiding the critical distinction to be made within both kingdoms which are actually constantly mixed in history, the doctrine became a religious theory for two separate dimensions of the world—church and state. Instead of applying the dialectic of law and gospel, the doctrine became a dualism according to which the law of retribution and compulsion ruled in the state and stood opposed to the rule of grace alone in the church.

If the law was thus separated from the gospel, then in the nineteenth century the state could soon be seen as presenting itself as a "law unto itself." In this way the state's monopoly of force and later the state politics of force were blessed. The more lawful and authoritative the state becomes, the purer and clearer the gospel of grace shines in the church. Bismarck was gladly celebrated as a "divine hero" of the worldly sphere. This separation of law and gospel in the nineteenth century, however, made the law graceless and the gospel lawless. Even today there are Lutherans who regret the repeal of the death penalty and, with that, the loss of the law of retribution. It was socialists such as the German Minister of Justice, Gustav Radbruch, who translated the Sermon on the Mount into the penal law and understood punishment no longer in terms of expiation but of resocialization.

2. An inversion of the two kingdoms doctrine arose when in the nineteenth century the distinction between the spiritual and the worldly regiment was replaced by the distinction between private and public, or inner and outer. With that, faith was made world-less and the world was made faith-less. God became unreal and reality God-less. The world was left to unfaith, and faith retired into the shell of the introspection of the pious soul. It was believed that the two kingdoms doctrine was realized in the schizophrenia of the modern mind.

3. The negative consequences of this misuse of the two kingdoms theory came to expression in Germany during the Hitler period. The doctrine provided no basis for religious and political resistance to Hitler's perversion of the state and the political religion of National Socialism. On the one hand, people bowed with holy timidity before the "autonomy" of the political power struggle; on the other hand, they welcomed the fascist "law and order" against the supposed chaos of democracy, liberalism, and the Enlightenment.[15] With this false separation of the two kingdoms, the gospel of the kingdom of Christ was made impotent on the one hand, and on the other, the right to arbitrariness was given over to the existing powers.

Two Basic Theological Questions.

1. The two kingdoms doctrine presents the gospel of Christ within an apocalyptic eschatology of the ongoing battle between

the kingdom of God and the kingdom of the devil. Is that correct? Must not the gospel of Jesus Christ begin from God's victory over the power of the devil in the cross and resurrection of Christ? Apocalyptic eschatology understands Christ from within the world-historical struggle of God against evil, but it fails to understand history and the end of history from the viewpoint of Christ. This is the questionable basic theological decision of the Lutheran two kingdoms theory; it begins with the struggle of faith with unfaith and of God with Satan but not from God's victory in Christ over sin, death, and the devil. For the two kingdoms doctrine this victory lies in the apocalyptic future, but not in the prophetic and apostolic perfect tense. Therefore, the worldly orders are seen only as powers of repression against evil until the end, but not as future-open processes for the justice and peace of God's kingdom.

2. The two kingdoms doctrine places the worldly regiment under the law. It remains unclear, however, what the context of this law is: the covenant of Israel, natural law, or the currently valid laws of a society? Meant for the most part are the currently valid laws which are then declared to be the laws of God—*tanquem ordinationes Dei* (as if they were the ordinances of God)! Lutherans therefore are called humorously the "eternal positivists." They seldom find criteria for the justice of the current laws. They find it easier to follow the positivistic principle, *auctoritas facit legem,* than the natural law principle, *veritas facit legem.* That often makes them blind over against the justice and injustice of current laws. They would rather view the gospel of grace in opposition to law and power than recognize in it the justice-creating character of the gospel.

3. Finally, as this presentation shows, the two kingdoms doctrine gives no criteria for a specific Christian ethics. It gives a criterion only for a recognition of a secular ethics or an ethics of the worldly orders. Basically, it is a theology of history but not a foundation for Christian ethics. It serves to sharpen the conscience; that is its strength. It brings into Christian ethics a realism which reckons with the given facts. But it does not motivate world-transforming hope. That is its weakness.

NOTES

1. Cf. G. Heidtmann, *Hat die Kirche geschwiegen? Das öffentliche Wort der Evangelischen Kirche in den Jahren 1945–1964* (Berlin, n.d.); W. Huber, *Kirche und Öffentlichkeit* (Stuttgart, 1973).

2. Cf. for this the most recent and thorough monograph by U. Duchrow, *Traditionsgeschichte und systematische Struktur der Zweireichelehre* (Stuttgart, 1970).

3. P. Althaus and J. Heckel, "Zwei-Reiche-Lehre," in *Evangelisches Kirchenlexikon*, 3, col. 1928–36 and 1937–45.

4. J. Heckel, *Lex Charitatis. Eine juristische Untersuchung über das Recht in der Theologie Martin Luthers* (Munich, 1953); idem, "Im Irrgarten der Zwei-Reiche-Lehre," *Theologische Existenz heute*, new series, no. 55 (Munich, 1957).

5. Günter Jakob, *Weltwirklichkeit und Christusglaube. Wider eine falsche Zwei-Reiche-Lehre* (Stuttgart, 1977).

6. Cf. with the following Duchrow, *Traditionsgeschichte*, 437ff.

7. Cf. now also H. A. Oberman, *Luther. Mensch zwischen Gott und Teufel* (Berlin, 1982), who gives strong emphasis to the apocalyptic structure of Luther's theology.

8. Gerhard Ebeling, "Die Notwendigkeit der Lehre von den zwei Reichen," in *Wort und Glaube* I (Tübingen, 1960), 407–28.

9. Ibid., 422.

10. Duchrow, *Traditionsgeschichte*, 526.

11. *WA*, 1, 463. For this see Ernst Wolf, "Politia Christi," in *Peregrinatio*, vol. 1 (Munich, 1954), 214f.

12. This quotation is a translation from O. Clemen, *Luthers Werke in Auswahl*, vol. 2 (Berlin, 1929), 360ff. The next two passages are taken from *Luther's Works*, vol. 45, ed. Walther I. Brandt (Philadelphia: Muhlenberg Press, 1962), 91, 92.

13. For example, G. Gloege, *Gnade für die Welt. Kritik und Krise des Luthertums* (Göttingen, 1964).

14. This is especially stressed by G. Törnvall, *Geistliches und weltliches Regiment bei Luther. Studien zu Luthers Weltbild und Gesellschaftsverständnis* (Munich, 1947); and E. Wolf, *Peregrinatio*, vol. 2: *Studien zur reformatorischen Theologie, zum Kirchenrecht und zur Sozialethik* (Munich, 1965).

15. In addition to E. Hirsch see also P. Althaus, *Theologie der Ordnungen*, 2d ed. (Gütersloh, 1935).

5

Barth's Doctrine of the Lordship of Jesus Christ and the Experience of the Confessing Church

The Calvinist Tradition

The teaching that the lordship of Christ already now permeates every area of life and thus calls Christians everywhere and without division into obedient discipleship is usually attributed to the Reformed tradition.[1] When it is called "Calvinist," the term is mostly critical. One points a warning finger at Calvin's alleged attempt to establish a *theocracy* in Geneva and at his fanatical intolerance of opponents. The public execution of the heretic Servetus is supposed to demonstrate the impossibility and unholiness of theocracy.

Or one points to the dangerous "politicization of French Protestantism" after 1560.[2] Until then the Huguenots had offered only passive resistance through suffering, martyrdom, and emigration, but after 1560 they turned to active resistance, using political and military means. The beginning of the end was the terrible St. Bartholomew's massacre of 1572. The end was the fall of the La Rochelle fortress in 1628.

Finally, reference is made to the Calvinist doctrine of the *right of resistance* against tyranny (Scottish Confession, Article 14) and to the Calvinist roots of modern democracy and capitalism. Thus, the Calvinist idea of theocracy seems to have a long and equivocal history. It has both its martyrs and its victims, its liberations and its oppressions.

The most important ways in which this Reformed tradition differs from the Lutheran tradition are the following:

1. The Lutheran Reformation began in principalities, while the Reformed church arose in the city-states of Zurich, Geneva, and Strasbourg. These city-states already had certain democratic forms in the constitutions of their municipal councils. Every Christian was at the same time a responsible citizen of his city. Here Reformation faith and political responsibility were, from the beginning, more closely intertwined than they were for the subjects of the principalities.

2. The basic concept of the *civitas Christiana* united faith and politics. In political discussions the citizenry always had to ask about God's will, whether in Zurich it was a question of the export of Swiss mercenaries to foreign lands, which Zwingli stopped with the help of the Bible—even today an acute point of irritation for Swiss weapons exporters—or in Geneva a question of the establishment of an Italian bank, which Calvin was against—in spite of Max Weber's thesis of the alliance between Calvinism and capitalism—and knew how to prevent. In the Zurich Disputations of 1523 Zwingli had already placed the politics of the city under the guiding principle of Christ: the ruling authority has "power and strength from Christ's teaching and action" (no. 35). One owes it obedience "as long as it asks nothing that is against God" (no. 38). "Should it become untrue, however, and outside the guiding principle of Christ (that is, the Sermon on the Mount), may it, with God's help, be deposed" (no. 42). Calvin also judged politics according to the lordship of God, as it is evident in the law of Moses and in the interpretation of this law by Christ.

3. Yet neither Zwingli nor Calvin wanted to establish "the kingdom of God on earth." Both of them, like Luther, distinguished divine and human justice. But they did not stress the contradiction and speak here about gospel and there about law; they asked, rather, about the connection between human justice and divine justice. The law is the "form of the gospel" (Barth), if it is the law of a gracious God. In both reformers we find certainly a *doctrine of two kingdoms*, in which faith and politics as well as church and state are kept separate, as in Luther. But both empha-

size also in politics the personal call to the *discipleship of Christ*. In the Reformed tradition the idea of discipleship has not become the "stepchild of Protestantism" (E. Wolf). According to the Reformed view, the Christian does not live simultaneously in two different worlds; he or she lives in the one encompassing lordship of Christ in the various relationships of this world.

4. In opposition to medieval clericalism, Luther had expounded the "general priesthood of all believers" and discovered thereby the right of the congregation. The Reformed tradition also discovered the "general kingship of all believers" and thus laid the cornerstone of modern democracy. Luther had in mind the clerical *tyrannis* in Rome. The West European Reformers saw the danger of the political *tyrannis* and discovered the political significance of the biblical idea of the covenant and of the constitution. "The crown does not rest on the head of a man," said John Milton. "The crown rests on the constitution of free citizens."[3]

The Confessing Church Under the Lordship of Christ

The impetus for today's doctrine of the "royal lordship of Christ" came from the theology of Karl Barth and the German church conflict in the time of Hitler.[4] Its basic formulations are found in the 1934 Barmen Theological Declaration, Theses 1 and 2:

Thesis 1: Jesus Christ, as he is testified to us in the Holy Scripture, is the one word of God, whom we are to hear, whom we are to trust and obey in life and in death.

We repudiate the false teaching that the church can and must recognize yet other happenings and powers, images and truths as divine revelation alongside this one Word of God, as a source of her preaching.

Thesis 2: Just as Jesus Christ is the pledge of the forgiveness of all our sins, just so—and with the same earnestness—is he also God's mighty claim on our whole life; in him we encounter a joyous liberation from the godless claims of this world to free and thankful service to his creatures.

We repudiate the false teaching that there are areas of our life in which we belong not to Jesus Christ but another lord, areas in which we do not need justification and sanctification through him.[5]

A short exposition of these theses of the Confessing Church will highlight the basic ideas.

All the confessions of the Reformation are essentially christocentric: the Christian church comes into its truth when Christ—and indeed Christ alone—is its Lord. The church comes into its freedom when it listens to the gospel of Christ—and indeed to that gospel alone—and to no other voice. Therefore all human church laws and all ordinances, rituals, and symbols of church tradition must be measured by the standard of the gospel of Christ.

The Confessing Church repeated this central confession in view of the totalitarian claims of state, nation, and society. Whenever political powers and economic and social interests want to make the church their servant, the lordship of Christ—indeed, the exclusive lordship of Christ over his church—must be confessed and publicly witnessed to through resistance. Only in the lordship of Christ can the church be free and have a liberating effect on people. It can never become a vassal of other powers and an accomplice of organized injustice without losing its identity.

Only through Christ and only through faith in deliverance through his gospel can people be freed from the godless and inhuman bondages of this world. There is no place in the world that is excepted and in which the liberating lordship of Christ is invalid. The experience of liberation from the godless chains of "this world" shows itself in thankful service to all of God's creatures. Therefore, the liberating power of Christ penetrates, redeems, and claims the whole of life, including its political and economic relationships. Those who would restrict the lordship of Christ to a spiritual, churchly, or private area, thus declaring other areas of life to be autonomous, deny fundamentally the lordship of Christ.

With these theses of the Barmen Declaration, the Confessing Church at first freed the church from the claims of state ideology and "political religion": "The church must remain the church." The first thesis rejected the German-Christian heresy that said: "Christ for the soul; Hitler for the people," or "the gospel for faith; the law of the German nation for ethics." In this area of church resistance to Hitler and his fascist religion the Confessing Church had success for a time, before it was worn down by its own battles of ecclesiastical disagreement.

The Confessing Church ran into difficulties, however, when the question of political resistance to Hitler became acute. After the war began, the second Barmen thesis led to conflicts of conscience. For then even confessing Christians marched into war for the divinely established authority, that is, for Hitler, although in faith they rejected him. One exception, among others, was Dietrich Bonhoeffer, who was driven by discipleship of Christ into political resistance and into conspiracy against Hitler.[6] There is still an unresolved discussion in German theology today as to whether resistance within the church is sufficient or if it must be broadened to political resistance.[7] Should Christians not react until the state reaches into the church itself and, for example, dismisses or arrests Jewish-Christian ministers or socialist priests? Or must they react as soon as socialists are persecuted, Jews murdered, and whole races or classes oppressed? How far does the liberating—and therefore also obligating—lordship of Christ reach?

Before we deal with these current questions, we must first clarify for ourselves the basic theological position that lies behind the doctrine of the all-embracing lordship of Christ.

The Basic Theological Position:
Christological Eschatology

The Barmen Theological Declaration begins with the assumption that in Christ God fully and finally revealed himself and that, therefore, there are no other sources of revelation for the church. God reveals himself in his Word, Jesus Christ. He does not reveal himself also in history, in nature, in political movements, or in political figures, which are understood to be in opposition to the revelation in Christ. God does not reveal himself ambiguously: he is unequivocal.

Consequently, Thesis 2 of the Barmen Declaration concludes that Jesus Christ is already Lord over the universe, over all powers, and thus over the whole of human life. Therefore, there are no areas in which the Christian must hear other powers and laws alongside the voice of Christ. All things and all relationships already now stand under the liberating and obligating lordship of Christ.

This basic theological position comes from the theology of Karl Barth. In three occasional publications he attempted during the years of the church conflict to understand the relationship between church and world christologically: "Gospel and Law" (1935); "Justification and Justice" (1938); "Christian Community and Civil Community" (1946).[8] The formulation of these three titles already indicates the direction of his thought: from Christ to church, from church to politics, from faith to life. The basic idea is clear: In Christ God humbled himself and accepted all human beings. He humbled himself even to death on the cross and accepted the whole misery, namely, the rejection of humanity. In Christ, however, God also exalted humanity and brought it to freedom and glory. Therefore, Christ is the reconciler of human beings who takes away their sin and condemnation. Because of this, Christ is also the victor over all powers and authorities. His resurrection from the dead and his exaltation to lordship reveal the triumph of God's grace. Death is already swallowed up in victory, and the exalted Lord leads all powers and authorities behind himself in a triumphal procession. For Barth three consequences followed.

1. The whole world is already objectively in Christ and under his lordship. No longer is there an apocalyptic struggle between the *regnum Dei* and the *regnum diaboli*. The conflict was decided once for all in the cross of Christ. The victory was revealed in the resurrection of Christ. Christian faith lives in the certainty of Christ's victory. As for this world, God has already decided for its salvation. Objectively, that is, from God's point of view, all human beings are already reconciled in Christ. Yet subjectively, that is, from the human point of view,[7] there are both the believers, who recognize their reconciliation, and the unbelievers, who do not. "Consciousness of God is one thing; being in God is something else" ("Christian Community"). Luther's *apocalyptic Christology* has been replaced by a *christological eschatology*.

Out of the constant *battle* between God and Satan comes God's *victory* over Satan, which in Christ has been won for humanity once and for all. Therefore, the eschatological future brings only the public and universal unveiling of this already accomplished victory of Christ.

2. If Christ is Lord, then all power in heaven and on earth is already given to him. Hence, it also follows that "the state as such originally and finally belongs to Jesus Christ, that its relatively independent substance, dignity, function, and objective are to serve the person and work of Jesus Christ and thus the justification of sinners that occurred in him" ("Justification"). For a long time Barth tried to prove this thesis with an untenable exegesis of Romans 13.[9] Günther Dehn believed that the *exousiai* (powers) named there are angelic powers. If all angels serve the exalted Lord, then political angelic powers are also subject to Christ. If that were so, then the consequence would be a christological metaphysic of the state. Later Barth dropped this exegesis. The theme of the New Testament is not a Christian metaphysics of the state, but a treatment of Christians' relationship to politics. It is not a theological doctrine of the state that is taught but a theological basis for discipleship of Christ in the area of politics.[10]

3. Above all, Barth noted that the New Testament describes the order of the new creation with political and not with religious concepts: kingdom of God (*basileia*), heavenly city (*polis*), heavenly citizenship (*politeuma*). Barth concludes that "the real earthly church sees its future and hope not in a heavenly reflection of its own existence, but precisely in the real heavenly state" ("Justification"). Not the eternal church, but the *polis* built by God and coming from heaven to earth is its promise and hope ("Christian Community"). Thus, the earthly, unfinished state and human, imperfect society are oriented toward the coming lordship of God. The Christian community makes this political eschatology apparent by living a consciously political existence.

The Christian professes that the world is no longer subject to demonic powers; in Christ it finds its freedom and its peace. Out of this faith there follows, therefore, the undivided responsibility of Christians and the church for the shaping of all areas of life, including the state, law, and the economic system. Because the lordship of Christ covers the whole world, the Christian recognizes his or her responsibility for it in discipleship to Jesus.

Thus in this basic theological position of Barth we find:

1. *Christological eschatology:* "Jesus is the victor." Christian faith everywhere lives in the certainty of Christ's victory.

2. *Universal Christology.* Christ is the Pantocrator: "For in him all things were created, in heaven and on earth, visible and invisible, whether thrones or dominions or principalities or authorities—all things were created through him and for him" (Col. 1:16). From this perspective, the historical struggles of the world are only the rearguard actions of an already defeated opponent.

3. The *christological ethics* of obedient discipleship in all areas of life, that is, an ethics of the relationship of created life to the reconciling God! According to which norms, however, and in which directions is the political discipleship of Christ to take place?

Christian Community and Civil Community

While strongly emphasizing their unity in basis and goal, Barth clearly distinguishes between church and state by speaking of two different communities. The church is the Christian community. It is the community of those people in one place who as Christians are especially called out from the rest by their knowledge of and for profession of Jesus Christ. The church becomes concrete in the "gathering of the faithful" (*ecclesia*). Its life is determined inwardly through the one faith, one love, and one hope, and outwardly through common confession and common proclamation of the gospel to all people.

The civil community is the community of all people in one place who are bound together by a common legal order. The purpose of their community is the securing of the outer, relative freedom of individuals and the outer, relative peace of their community and, to this extent, the preservation of the basic humanity of their lives.

It is important that Barth characterized the civil community as a community of law (covenant) and not first as the authority with a monopoly on force. Justice, not force, is the foundation of the state, even when adherence to the law is compelled by force. In the civil community are Christians and non-Christians together, although set apart regionally, that is, nationally. In the Christian community only the faithful are together, yet in ecumenical universality in all nations. The Christian community is held together by the consciousness of God, but in the civil community the relationship to God cannot be an element of the legal order.

The Christian community recognizes the necessity of an essentially different civil community. It recognizes the legal order and the necessity of its protection through force and sees there a divine ordering, a constancy of divine providence vis-à-vis human sin, and an instrument of divine grace. The civil community has with the Christian community both a common origin and a common goal. Hence, it is an order of the divine grace to the extent that this grace, in its relationship to the still unredeemed world, also signifies the continuing patience of God. The civil community is a sign that God does not abandon the world to itself, but preserves it from chaos in relative freedom. It gives humanity time for the proclamation of the gospel and time for faith. Apart from the kingdom of Christ, the civil community has no existence based upon and developing according to its own destiny. It is, rather—outside the church but not beyond the domain of the lordship of Jesus Christ—"an exponent of his kingdom." When the Christian community, according to Barmen Thesis 5, recognizes "with thanks and reverence toward God the benevolence, of this, his provision," it follows that there can be no indifferent, apolitical Christianity.

But how should the Christian community affect the civil community politically? Against the dissolution of Christianity into a political movement of the right or left, Barth always maintained that "the church must remain the church." The church affects the civil community precisely because it is the church of Jesus Christ and concentrates entirely on its Lord.

Barth used the image of two concentric circles to represent the relationship between the Christian community and the civil community. The Christian community is the inner circle of the kingdom of Christ. It proclaims the liberating lordship of Christ and the hope of the coming kingdom of God. Even the best of all possible civil communities does not do that. Precisely in the fulfilling of its own task the Christian community also joins in the task of the civil community, but indirectly, as it were. When the church believes in and proclaims Jesus Christ, it believes in and proclaims him who, as head of his church, is also Lord of the world. When it proclaims the kingdom of God, it validates all political concepts vis-à-vis its hope, but also its critique. This is true especially for political realities.

First, the church's proclamation will destroy the human hubris present in all political ideologies and lordships and clearly point to the eschatologically provisional character of all political processes. But it will also resist the resignation inherent in political actions and spread the hope for the eschatological fulfillment of politics in the city of God. Nevertheless, the proclamation of the church can erect no Christian doctrine of the state nor religiously justify and bless political conditions. Thus, by concentrating on the proclamation of Christ as Lord, the Christian community keeps political processes in operation and open to the kingdom of God. Politics on earth remains an imperfectible process for freedom and justice. Whoever tries to perfect this process politically becomes a tyrant; whoever resigns in this process delivers the world to the tyrants. Barth seems to see the indirect effect of Christ's proclamation and the Christian community on the civil community in the fact that political situations remain changeable and political changes are kept historically imperfectible. The church does not divinize politics, but it does not demonize politics either. It brings politics humanly into the suspension of permanent improvability and historical imperfectibility. This is the first step.[11]

From this suspension, into which the civil community is brought by the Christian community through its proclamation and existence, there follows for Barth a second step: are there directions and guidelines for Christian decisions that are to be implemented in the political sphere? The state is not the kingdom of

God and never will be. Nonetheless, even it stands under the promise of the coming kingdom of God. How is this to be understood?

Barth uses the language of parable for this suspension between identity and difference. The state cannot be equated with the kingdom of God, but the two are not totally dissimilar either. But in between there is parable: "In the Christian view, the justification of the state is its existence as parable, as analogy, as corresponding entity for the kingdom of God believed in and proclaimed by the church." Politics, like culture, is capable of and in need of this parable with the kingdom of God.

For this reason Barth calls the civil community the outer circle of Christ's kingdom. Now, since the Christian community as the inner circle and the civil community as the outer circle have their common center in Christ the Lord and their common goal in the kingdom of God, the Christian community will always, through its political decisions, strive to have political justice correspond as a parable to God's justice, not contradict it. The Christian community wants the state to point toward the kingdom of God, not away from it. It wants God's grace also to be reflected in the external, temporary dealings of the political community.

How is this to happen? Barth gives some examples.

1. Life in the Christian community is based on the reality of God's becoming human. Thus, as far as that community is concerned, the state and the law exist for the sake of human beings, not human beings for the sake of the state and the law. Since God became human, the human being is supposed to be the measure of all things political. Therefore, Barth turns against the insatiable monster of nationalism and against the dehumanizing fetish of capitalism.

2. The Christian community is witness to the divine justification of human beings. It will therefore follow the political principle that "right makes might" and step in against anarchy and tyranny.

3. The Christian community is witness to the Son of man, who came to seek that which is lost. Politically it will step in for the lost, the weak, the poor, the threatened. From among the various

social possibilities, it will choose the one from which it expects the highest degree of social justice.

4. The Christian community is called to the freedom of God's children. Thus it will become involved politically in human and civil rights. "It will not under any circumstance support a practical dictatorship or a partial or temporary limitation of civil freedoms, and will under all circumstances oppose the principle of dictatorship."

5. The Christian community lives from the light of the public revelation of God in Christ. The corresponding necessary political consequence of this consists in the fact that the Christian community is the unrelenting opponent of all secret politics and secret diplomacy. Where freedom and responsibility are united in service to the civil community, words can and must be open to all ears, and actions to all eyes.

In this essay ("Community") Barth consciously limited himself to examples of Christian political decisions in order to make clear his basic thought: politics is capable of and needs to be a parable of the lordship of Christ that is believed in the Christian community and proclaimed by it. This requires of the church, however, that "the true state must have its model and example in the true church. Thus the church exists in an exemplary way, that is, so that simply by its being there and being itself, it is also a source of renewal and strength for the preservation of the state." The proclamation of the church would be in vain if the church were not the first to begin by its life, its constitution, and its government and administration to witness in a practical way to this lordship of Christ.

In summary let us stress the following:

1. The Christian community and the civil community have different commissions in history, but they have their common foundation in Christ the Lord and their common goal in the kingdom of God. Therefore, it is not enough to point out their differences; one must, because of their common foundation and common structure, seek out correspondences, parables, and analogies.

2. The state is regarded, not as God's necessary force against evil, but as an outer, earthly, and temporary vessel for the good.

It is not understood only as a repressive power against chaos and sin as it is in part in Luther and clearly in Lutheranism. Understood as the civil community and the legal community of justice, it contains the positive possibilities of a parable of the kingdom of God.

3. Whereas according to Lutheran doctrine the Christian in the worldly regiment is required to act politically only according to the principles of reason, expediency, and love of neighbor, Barth provides, with help from his parable theory, substantial criteria and guidelines for Christian political action. The Christian faith not only frees political reason to be itself with its own rationality, as the Lutherans say, but it also lays claim on political reason through its interest in making parables for the kingdom of God visible already here on earth.

4. Barth's *political parable theory* is often ridiculed on the basis of his example of the necessary Christian rejection of secret politics and secret diplomacy. "It is immediately clear that this argumentation is theologically and politically untenable."[12] One also gets the impression that the examples were chosen arbitrarily and that the analogies were developed only by example and in a playful manner. Barth was also criticized for failing to recognize the problem of "relative autonomy" and lack of accountability in the political arena. But if one reads his essay closely and asks what is the total view of politics behind it, one discovers the basic elements of democratic socialism as the precursor and the relatively best available correspondence to the lordship of Christ and the kingdom of God. Precisely within this framework Barth calls for the public transparency of all political discussions and decisions. This is a fundamental democratic requirement of socialism[13] that is immediately evident, theologically and politically.

5. For Barth, democratic socialism was not the kingdom of God on earth. Nor would it ever be. But it was for Barth and indeed can be the best present—and hence provisional—political parable of the kingdom of God. Barth's opting for democratic socialism was never simply affirmative: "Christians for socialism"; rather, it was always critical at the same time, "Socialism for the sake of the kingdom of God," but only to the extent that

socialism corresponds to the kingdom of God and does not contradict it.

Evaluation and Critique

Let us try again with great care to present a model for the doctrine of the lordship of Christ in the Christian community and the civil community:

Center

God in Christ
Christ the Lord
↓

Christian Community
faith—proclamation—prayer
↓

Civil Community
capable of and in need of parable:
1. for the sake of human beings   2. rights of the weak
3. human right of freedom   4. public politics and the like
↓

Common Goal
Kingdom of God, heavenly city on earth
Finality of faith in Christ the Pantocrator
Provisionality of all earthly political processes

Misuses. Because of its simplicity, this model is hard to protect from misuse. Barth's ordering of the church before the state and society can easily lead to clerical guardianship, whether theologically from the right or the left. His demand that the Christian community be an example for the civil community can only be met by a church that is what he calls "the true church." *But where is the true church?* The actual church, with its feudal constitution, its anachronistic symbols and rites, and its outdated language is in most cases less like the forerunner of the civil community than it is the taillight of cultural development. If the possibility and power to create parables of the lordship of Christ in political life depend on the preeminence and example of the Christian community, then Barth's parable theory fails miserably in practice.

How, for example, can the Catholic church be against secret politics and demand the transparency of political negotiations and processes when its own Congregation of Faith does not even hold to the fundamental principles of current legal practice and does not even keep the accused informed—to say nothing at all of the public? How can a German Protestant church take the side of democracy in public life when it rejects the democratization of its own constitution and is not based on the "right of the congregation"? Barth knew, of course, the condition of the churches, and he also is critical of them at the end of his essay. But he should have begun with this critique in order not to become theologically illusory.

Two Critical Questions about Theological Foundations. 1. The doctrine of the lordship of Christ over the Christian community and the civil community is based on christological eschatology: *Christ is the Pantocrator* who already rules over heaven and earth. This Christology was first powerfully proclaimed in early Christian hymns and then in Ephesians and Colossians. These hymns actually proclaim the already initiated *lordship of Christ over the world* and the already accomplished subjugation of cosmic and political powers. Therefore, in doxological jubilation Christians already participate in the universal lordship of Christ. They are themselves already raised with Christ. They share in his *resurrected* lordship. They already *rule* with him. But this, according to Ernst Käsemann, is an enthusiastic congregational piety that forgets the crucified one and retreats from earthly reality.[14]

Paul constantly fought against this so-called Corinthian enthusiasm and repeatedly taught that the lordship of Christ can be none other than the lordship of the crucified one. In the present Christians have an immediate part in the cross but not an immediate part in the resurrection glory of Christ. The certainty of the victory of faith is a certainty only *under the cross* and nowhere else. Indeed, Barth seldom speaks of the "kingly" lordship of Christ, restricting himself to talk of "the lordship of Christ." It must be stressed, however, against the language of his students and in part against Barth himself, that the lordship of Christ does not resemble that of a *king* but is the lordship of the crucified one, who conquers not through great power but through weakness and rules through his vicarious suffering on the cross.

Without the living memory of the cross and passion of Christ, the doctrine of the kingly lordship of Christ becomes triumphalist and theocratic. It becomes self-justifying. But Christ is no su-perking—king of kings—and also no superstar; he is the Son of man, whose "power is made perfect in weakness" (2 Cor. 12:9).[15] The memory of the crucified one is presumably related to the fact that Paul does not confer the title of Cosmocrator on the resur-rected and now ruling Christ, and that the assertion that all king-doms and powers of this world are subject to Christ is transposed from the perfect tense of the hymns into the future of his hope. According to 1 Cor. 15:28, God *will* make everything subject to his Christ and then the Son *will* turn over the kingdom to the Father. That Christ is Lord meant for Paul that "he *must* reign until he has put all of his enemies under his feet" (1 Cor. 15:25). Not until *then,* when the lordship of the crucified one becomes the lordship of God, will all earthly lordships, authorities, and powers, together with death, *then* be destroyed.[16]

Thus, what for Barth has *already* been accomplished in the cross and resurrection of Christ, for Paul has *not yet* happened, according to Käsemann. What for Barth is the certainty of victory is for Paul the certainty of the Christian's hope.

2. Barth's doctrine of the already present lordship of Christ over all principalities, authorities, and powers leads to the follow-ing ambiguity: either all powers, including states, serve now al-ready the Pantocrator Christ, whether they know it or not; or else the Pantocrator rules over Christians and only through them rules all the stately domains of this world. Then his lordship reaches as far as the obedience of the faithful reaches.

In "Justification and Justice" Barth says, "The preaching of justification as preaching of the kingdom of God already here and now establishes true justice and the *true state*." That viewpoint leads to a Christian metaphysic of the state. In "Christian Community and Civil Community," however, he says, "The Christian community is not in a position to set up a teaching as the Christian doctrine of the *just state*."

If there were a Christian doctrine of the state, based on the lordship of Christ over the world, it would be difficult, with 1 Cor. 15:26, to expect the destruction of all lordship, authority, and power from the fulfillment of Christ's lordship. Hence, the post-Barthian discussion in Germany has generally drawn back from the theological foundation of the state. The lordship of Christ reaches according to our experience as far as human beings, freed from sin by his death, are obedient to it. One can well derive from his lordship directives for the political discipleship of Christians in political life but not a metaphysics of the state that is equally valid for Christians and non-Christians. Christocratic ethics can only be discipleship ethics. It is ethics for Christians but not Christian ethics for the state. It is political ethics of the Christian community but not Christian politics of the civil community.

NOTES

1. For historical literature see W. Köhler, *Huldrych Zwingli* (Leipzig, 1943); Fr. Wendel, *Calvin, Sources et Évolution de sa Pensée Religieuse* (Strasbourg, 1950); J. T. McNeill, *The History and Character of Calvinism* (New York: Oxford University Press, 1954); W. Haller, *The Rise of Puritanism* (New York: Harper and Row, 1957); A. A. van Schelven, *Het Calvinisme gelurende zijn Bloeitijd*, 1 and 2 (Amsterdam, 1951).

2. R. Nürnberger, *Die Politisierung des französischen Protestantismus* (Tübingen, 1948).

3. J. Bohatic, *England und die Geschichte der Menschen- und Bürgerrechte* (Graz, 1956).

4. E. Wolf, *Barmen, Kirche zwischen Versuchung und Gnade* (Munich, 1957).

5. The text is found in *Bekenntnisschriften und Kirchenordnungen der nach Gottes Wort reformierten Kirche,* ed. W. Niesel (Zurich, 1938), 333ff.

6. See E. Bethge, *Dietrich Bonhoeffer: Theologian, Christian, Con-*

temporary (London: Collins, 1970); E. Feil, *Die Theologie Dietrich Bonhoeffers. Hermeneutik, Christologie, Weltverständnis* (Mainz, 1971); J. Moltmann, "Herrschaft Christi und soziale Wirklichkeit nach D. Bonhoeffer," ThEx NF 71 (Munich, 1959).

7. See E. Bethge, "Über das Erbe der Bekennenden Kirche, Wissenschaft und Praxis in Kirche und Gesellschaft," 60th yr., vol. 4 (1971): 149–61; A. Burgsmüller, ed., *Zum politischen Auftrag der christlichen Gemeinde, Barmen II. Votum des Theol. Ausschusses der Evangelischen Kirche der Union* (Gütersloh, 1974).

8. K. Barth, *Community, Church, and State: Three Essays* (New York: Doubleday, 1960). In this edition the second essay, "Justification and Justice," is entitled "Church and State." In *Church Dogmatics*, vol. 4, 1–4, Barth develops Christology in detail within the framework of the doctrine of redemption.

9. Concerning exegesis see A. Strobel, "Zum Verständnis von Römer 13," ZNW 47 (1956): 67–93; E. Käsemann, "Römer 13 in unserer Generation," ZThK 56 (1959): 316–76.

10. Karl Barth's friend Ernst Wolf has shown in a number of publications that for Christians the idea of the kingly lordship of Christ cannot result in a metaphysic of the state, but only in a doctrine of political virtue: "Was heißt Königsherrschaft Christi heute?" (1961); "Königsherrschaft Christi und lutherische Zwei-Reiche-Lehre," (1964); "Schöpferische Nachfolge?" (1960).

11. That point is especially stressed by W.-D. Marsch, "Gerechtigkeit im Tal des. Todes," in *Theologie zwischen Gestern und Morgen. Interpretationen und Anfragen zum Werk Karl Barths* (Munich, 1968), 167–91.

12. Thus W. Huber, *Kirche und Öffentlichkeit* (Stuttgart, 1972), 463, following H. Thielicke, *Theologische Ethik*, vol. 2 (Tübingen, 1968), 714.

13. This was recently demonstrated again in Fr. W. Marquardt, *Theologie und Sozialismus. Das Beispiel Karl Barths* (Mainz, 1971) and accepted in H. Gollwitzer, "Reich Gottes und Sozialismus bei Karl Barth," ThEx NF 169 (Munich, 1972).

14. Käsemann, "Römer 13."

15. See J. Moltmann, *The Crucified God* (New York: Harper and Row, 1974).

16. Ibid., "Trinity and Eschatology."

6

Political Theology and Political Hermeneutic of the Gospel

What Is Political Theology?
What Does It Want?

The Lutheran two kingdoms doctrine arose out of the Reformation. The Reformation happened four hundred years ago in the power of the newly discovered gospel and was related to the medieval *corpus Christianum*. It had immediate consequences for the relationship of church and state to one another and for the life of Christians in both.

The new lordship of Christ doctrine arose out of the resistance of the Confessing Church. This resistance lived out of the power of the gospel and was related to the modern secularized state and the anti-Christian, totalitarian ideology of the state.

In postwar Germany the effect of the Confessing Church was repressed by the restoration of the old church-state relationships. In place of a free church in a free state there arose a new institutionalized partnership between the established churches and the state which was secured through church contracts (on the Protestant side) and concordats (on the Roman Catholic side). The churches fulfilled the stabilizing and ideological functions of civil religion desired by the state and society, and in return the state and society gave privileges to the churches. The romantic idea of the "Christian West" encompassed the churches, the state, the schools, and society. This "utopia of the status quo" was attractive in the Federal Republic of Germany from 1945 until the be-

97

ginning of the 1960s because many people after their experience of the chaos of war sought only order and security.

The new concept of a political theology has arisen out of a deep dissatisfaction with this restoration of antiquated conditions in Germany. In contrast to Barth, it began with criticism and a new definition of the social and political functions of the church under the conditions of the modern age.

In Germany this concept was the first attempt at a theology critically related to society in which Catholic and Protestant theologians participate collaboratively. Political theology therefore has a transconfessional character and is ecumenical insofar as both churches stand before the same problem of the growing irrelevance of their doctrines for modern life, finding in none of the different theological-church traditions the *key* for the solution of the problems of the modern age.[1]

This new political-critical theology for the church and Christian life under the conditions of the European modern age has two starting points.

First, the process of secularization has not yet received a sufficient theological answer or explanation. Political theology has taken up the Marxist criticism of religion in this process.[2] This is, as is well known, not a criticism of the content of Christian theology and religious faith but only a functional criticism, a criticism of the social, political, and psychological functions of religion and church. It is no longer asked whether a theological doctrine is true or false; instead, the doctrine is tested practically to see whether its effects are oppressive or liberating, alienating or humanizing. With this method, praxis becomes the criterion of truth. This criterion is true not only for Marx; it also is operative from Kant to Sartre; it is the characteristic feature of the modern spirit. With this criterion, reflective consciousness no longer has an intuitive contemplative relationship to reality but instead has won an operative and therefore self-critical relationship to reality.

A theology which enters upon this way must therefore reflect constantly and critically upon its practical functions as well as upon its content. A church which engages in this mode of theology may no longer ask abstractly about the relationship of church and politics, as if these were two separate things which must be brought together; rather, this church must begin with a critical awareness of its own political existence and its actual social functions.

Political theology is not a new dogmatic. Rather it wants on the level of fundamental theology to awaken the political consciousness of every Christian theology. There is theology which is conscious of its own political function; there is also naive and, as it were, politically unconscious theology. But there is no *a*political theology; neither in earth nor in heaven. There are churches that do not want publicly to recognize their political *Sitz im Leben* within their society. They conceal, cover, and disguise it, then assert that they are politically "neutral"—something which they *de facto* never are. There are Christian groups which exist politically consciously as Christian groups. But there is no *a*political church, neither in history nor in the kingdom of God. Political theology does not want to make political instead of theological questions the central concern of theology but, rather, the reverse. It wants to be thoroughly Christian in the political functions of theology. It does not want to politicize the church, but it does want to Christianize church politics and the political involvement of Christians. It therefore takes up the modern functional criticism of religion and urges movement from the orthodoxy of faith to the orthopraxis of discipleship of Christ.

Second, the history of the modern age will not be understood if we view it theologically as only negative and speak of the "modern emancipation from tradition," the "secularization of the holy," or the "defection of the world from God." Modern consciousness criticizes the past and the traditions regarding origins because it is oriented toward the future and wants to organize human life for the project of history.[3]

The criticism of past reality takes place in the name of past and present possibilities for the future. The criticism of origins serves the future. The criticism of tradition and institutions seeks freedom for the new. Thus, Kant was the first to put the modern question to religion: "What may I hope for?" The experience of transcendence is shifted with this question from metaphysics into eschatology.

Following the primacy of love in medieval theology and the

primacy of faith in Reformation theology, the modern age disclosed the primacy of hope. Immanence is no longer experienced as the transient earth under an immutable heaven, but as an open process of life and as the history of a still unknown future.

For one hundred and fifty years theology and church did not understand this modern primacy of the future and the modern struggle for the truth of hope. Because both theology and the church encountered this development in forms of criticism of the church and of social revolution, they felt forced into a defensive posture and allied themselves with antirevolutionary powers and conservative ideologies. They saw the future of the modern age simply as the image of the antichrist and its hope as the spirit of blasphemy. Only recently have we learned to understand that the modern situation calls us to "account for the hope that is in us" (1 Pet. 3:15). This accounting is no longer achieved theologically with the small treatise on the moral virtues in which hope is dealt with very narrowly. Rather, this accounting requires a new eschatological orientation of the whole of Christian theology in order that theology can respond with the biblical promissory history to the modern interest in the history of the future.

The new political theology therefore has declared eschatology, which has hitherto been handled mostly apocryphally, as the foundation and medium of Christian theology. It has projected Christian theology as messianic theology. The roots of political theology in Europe lie in "the theology of hope."[4]

The Basic Theological Position: Eschatological Christology[5]

When one speaks of Christology, it sounds specifically Christian, but it is really not so. The doctrine of the Christ is the doctrine of the anointed Messiah, the hoped-for liberator, and the awaited divine redeemer. Christology is nothing other than messiology. There is also Jewish and Islamic messianism and messiology. There is messiology in every doctrine of salvation and every liberation ideology.

The modern age also has developed its political messianisms. Nationalism declared the nation to be the messiah; Italian fascism spoke of the Duce of the end time; German National Socialism worshiped the Führer of a Third, or Thousand Year, Reich; Saint Simon called the machine messiah because it would liberate us from toil and work; and in early Marxism the proletariat who freed themselves became the "redeemed redeemer" of the world. Everywhere in the modern age the primacy of the future was recognized and people themselves organized the end of history. Political and social revolutionary messianism arose as a result.

But if Christology is messiology, then the peculiar and distinctive element of this messianic Christology does not lie in its orientation toward the future, nor simply in a present liberation from misery, but in the definition of the *subject:* Who is the Christ? Who is the Messiah? Christian Christology believes that the Christ is not a nation, a Führer, a people, or a spirit but Jesus of Nazareth—the one sent with the gospel of the kingdom to the poor, crucified under Pontius Pilate, raised from the dead by God, and coming to judge the living and the dead. The specifically Christian is not Christology as such, but Jesus.

But if Christian theology really wants to understand Jesus as the true Christ, it must grasp him and his history in an eschatological way. It must read the story of Jesus within the framework of the Old Testament promissory history in order to understand his conflict with the law and his fulfillment of the Old Testament promises. It must so interpret his death and his resurrection from the dead in the light of hope in the coming God in order to understand him as the liberator of the world sent from God. Jesus is understood historically only if his story is read in light of the remembered hope of the Old Testament and the awakened hope of the kingdom of God. In this way then he is understood as God's Christ.

This brings us then to the very old Christ-question put by the Jewish people: "Are you the coming one or shall we wait for another?" The religious question of modern times is: "What may I hope for?" This second question is very similar to the Jewish question. "The coming one" was a symbol simultaneously for the messianic liberator and for God himself. Jesus' well-known answer to John the Baptist's question was, "Go and tell John what you see and hear: the blind see, the lame walk, lepers are cleansed and the deaf hear; the dead are raised up and the poor have good news proclaimed to them. And blessed is he who takes no offense at me" (Matt. 11:4–6). Similarly, Luke summarizes the messianic mission of Jesus: "The Spirit of the Lord is upon me, because he has anointed me to preach good news to the poor. He has sent me to proclaim release to the captives and recovering of sight to the blind, to set at liberty those who are oppressed, to proclaim the acceptable year of the Lord" (Luke 4:18ff.). The universal question about the future concentrates here on the question of the "coming one" who will turn calamity to wholeness of salvation and lead people from oppression to freedom.

If Jesus shows himself to be the coming one through his gospel to the poor, his healing of the sick, and his forgiveness of sinners, and, if he is believed in and known as the coming one by those people who are affected, then the whole future of salvation and the kingdom of freedom must be expected from him. Where the poor hear the gospel through him, where the blind recover their sight through him, where the lame walk, where the oppressed are set free, and sins are forgiven, there he reveals himself as the Christ because he makes present their true future.

Jesus' messianic message and deeds may be summarized by the concept of messianic anticipation: through him and in his way "the kingdom of God has come near," so that already his healing, liberating, and saving actions can be experienced now. Through him and in him the end of history is already present in the midst of history in a hidden way. We can therefore summarize the many diverse messianic titles found in the New Testament by saying, "Jesus—anticipator of the kingdom of God" (Jesus—*Anticipator regni Dei*).[6]

But if Jesus is the anticipator of God, then he must simultaneously and unavoidably become the sign of resistance to the powers of a world which contradicts God and to the laws of a world which is closed to the future. Because he proclaimed the kingdom of God to the poor, he came into conflict with the rich. Because he gave the grace of God to sinners, he contradicted the laws of the pious, the Pharisees, and the Zealots. Because he revealed God's lordship to the lowly and oppressed, Pilate let him be crucified in the name of the Roman Caesar-god. Thus eschatological anticipation inevitably brings forth historical resistance. Salvation can enter the situation of misery in no other way; liberation can enter into a world of oppression in no other way.

If we read the story of Jesus in the light of his resurrection and of the coming God, we know this more clearly: God raised him from the dead. This means that the universal "resurrection of the dead" has already begun in this one. The end time has already broken in. The future of the new creation has already begun. Because people have faith in and recognize the risen Messiah, God's people of the end time assemble in expectation of the coming kingdom of God. Jesus' resurrection from the dead must be understood as eschatological anticipation and as the real beginning of the resurrection process and the world's new creation of the end time (Rom. 8:11). Thus, in the New Testament the resurrected one is called "the first fruits of those who have fallen asleep" (1 Cor. 15:20) and "the author of life" (Acts 3:15). Through Jesus' resurrection the ambiguous and indefinite expectation of the resurrection of the dead for judgment becomes an unambiguous and certain hope in the kingdom of God and eternal life. Out of this stance of waiting comes also the practical passion to renew life now in the spirit of resurrection and no longer to accommodate to the system of this world.

Indeed, this Easter anticipation is also related to resistance, namely, to the cross of Christ and to the cross which Christians are to carry.

Whom did God raise from the dead? The condemned blasphemer, the crucified rebel, the abandoned Son of God. The future of God and of salvation—the kingdom of God and God's kingdom of freedom—is therefore recognizable and realized nowhere other than in the poor and violated Jesus, crucified for us.

But this means that through his suffering he liberates those who are suffering; through his weakness he gains power in the world; through his God-forsakenness he brings God to the forsaken; through his death he creates salvation for those condemned to death.

The lordship of Christ is no royal, "kingly" lordship (Barth) but the lordship of the obedient servant of God (Philippians 2), the friendship of the Lamb of God (Revelation). Nor is the lordship of Christ a world-denying religious rule.[7] It is rather the rule of the real bodily crucified one in the midst of this world. He rules by serving. He redeems through suffering. He liberates the world from death through his representative death. The unity of the risen and the crucified one is grasped neither by a two kingdoms doctrine nor by the doctrine of the kingly lordship of Christ, but only by an eschatological Christology, a Christology "from ahead."

In saying this we are already engaged in criticism of both Luther and Barth.

1. Although Luther related his theology of the cross critically to the church and to faith so that it was also liberating, he left the social and political consequences to Karlstadt, Müntzer, and others whom he declared and condemned "enthusiasts." In Protestantism that judgment led to interpreting the lordship of the crucified one as intended only for the inner justification of the heart. Political theology, however, begins from the assumption—to speak with J. B. Metz—that the effects of his death belong not to the privacy of religiosity but rather, as Hebrews says, "outside" the gate of the city.[8] The salvation which faith embraces in hope is therefore not a private but a *public* salvation, not only spiritual but also bodily, not a purely religious but also a political salvation. We may not separate this into two kingdoms but must recognize the cruciform character of this Savior and his salvation in all dimensions of life.

2. With his doctrine of the Pantocrator Christ, Barth, on the other hand, fell into a kind of enthusiasm. The lordship of Jesus Christ in the shape of the cross is devoured in this world. Hope is not devoured but rather holds open the cruciform lordship of Christ. But as Hebrews says, "As it is, we do not yet see everything in subjection to him" (2:8). Ernst Käsemann described this Pauline "not yet" as the "eschatological proviso."[9] Certainly the crucified one is already the Lord in his person, but he is, as such, still on the way to his lordship overall. He draws the faithful into his way toward the fulfillment. This eschatological provisionality

is the historical form of the lordship of the crucified one and of Christian existence. The theology of the cross is always a theology on the way and, conversely, the theology on the way is a theology of the cross. Thus the Christian hope leads to conflict, contradiction, and suffering. It will become certain of victory only *in* this struggle, not apart from it and certainly not in flight from it! Consequently every truly eschatological theology must become a political theology, that is, a socially critical theology.

Political Hermeneutic

The Messianic Hermeneutic of History. "Hermeneutic" is the art of interpreting texts. Every interpretation has two sides, a historical and a prophetic side; it includes historical explication and prophetic application. One must ascertain by means of historical-critical research what words, sentences, stories, and symbols meant in their own time. One also must understand prophetically what they mean in our time. Hermeneutic is, therefore, the art of translation from the past into the present.

But why should we *re*-present the past at all? Whence arises the interest which guides such knowledge? The past does not have to be re-presented simply for the sake of its pure pastness. Nor does it have to be repeated merely to give the present a firm ground of tradition. Only when there is something in the past that points beyond itself into the future is there any point in remembering the past. The past in its unfulfilled character, its future-oriented direction, and its primal nature presses upon the present because it seeks its fulfillment and completion. Hermeneutic returns to the witnesses of the past because it seeks the future in this past.[10] History is "hope in the mode of remembrance."

Christian hermeneutic then reads the Bible as witness of God's promissory history and the human history of hope. The interest which guides its knowledge is an interest in the power of the future and how this is revealed in God's promises and stirred in human hope. Because God's promissory history, about which the Bible in its core speaks, has again and again liberated people from their inner and outer prisons—Israel from Egypt, Jesus from death, and the church from the nations—the remembrance of this story is thus as dangerous as it is liberating for every present moment; dangerous for the powerful, but liberating for the powerless. By looking backward from our present to this history, we also learn to see critically beyond our own present.

With this perspective we are already in the prophetic dimension of hermeneutic: "Past things become present in order to announce the things of the future" (Augustine). Karl Löwith called the historian a prophet who is turned backward. We can expand this insight and call the prophet a historian who is turned ahead. As the historian discovers hope in the mode of memory, so the prophet shapes memory in the mode of hope. For the "power of the future," anticipated in the biblical history of promise, stretches far beyond the present and its given possibilities. To grasp this in hope means to become free. We then understand history as a whole as the element of the future. What we call the past are anticipations of the future which have preceded us. When we orient our present toward this future, it becomes a new frontline of this future. Then history is no longer the time of death and of what is past; it is rather the time of the future.

When we speak in such an absolute and dominant way of "the" future which defines all history and therefore does not itself pass away, *God* is meant as the power of the future. The power of his future affects people in such a way that they are liberated from the compulsion to repeat the past and from bondage to the givenness of what is already there. To speak of the history of this future means to speak of the history of human liberation. That is the basic thinking then of the eschatologically oriented hermeneutic of history.

Political Hermeneutic: Knowing History by Participating in History. Political hermeneutic links up with eschatological hermeneutic. Earlier hermeneutic usually remained at one level: from text to text, from understanding to understanding, from faith to faith. When hermeneutic, however, involves a promissory history, then the way of interpretation goes from promise to fulfillment. When it involves a history of hope, then interpretation goes from expectation to realization. When it involves the remembrance of liberation, then the way goes from oppression to free-dom, that is, hermeneutic does not remain on the intellectual theoretical level, but wants to lead, by way of the experience of understanding hope, to a new praxis of hope. In this regard, the eleventh thesis of Karl Marx against Feuerbach is pertinent: "The philosophers have only interpreted the world; the point, however, is to transform it."

If the remembered promise for the liberation of people and for the humanizing of their relationships is pressed, then the reverse of this thesis is also true: Everything depends upon interpreting these transformations critically. The way of political hermeneutic cannot go one-sidedly from reflection to action. That would be pure idealism. The resulting action would become blind. Instead, this hermeneutic must bind reflection and action together, thus requiring reflection in the action as well as action in the reflection.

The hermeneutical method to which this leads is called in the ecumenical discussion "the action-reflection method." Christian hope motivates those who hope for the liberating act of love. The historical practice of liberation, however, must be reflected upon and criticized in its effects and consequences in the light of this hope.

To say this differently: Without personal participation in the apostolic mission and without cooperation with the kingdom of God, one cannot understand the Bible. And without understand-ing the Bible one cannot participate in the mission of the aposto-late, nor can one cooperate with the kingdom of God in the world.

Political hermeneutic is experienced in Christian passion and action. In political activity and suffering one begins to read the Bible with the eyes of the poor, the oppressed, and the guilty—and to understand it. Such a theology "does not stop with reflect-ing on the world, but rather tries to be part of the process through which the world is transformed. It is a theology which is open . . . to the gift of the kingdom of God."[11]

Political hermeneutic therefore rejects pure theory in theology just as it does blind activism in ethics. Its model is a differentiated theory-praxis relationship in which theory and praxis, thinking and doing, mutually drive each other forward. Theory and prac-

RESPONSIBILITY FOR THE WORLD AND CHRISTIAN DISCIPLESHIP

tice do not belong in two different kingdoms. However, they never wholly correspond with each other. They do not come to a unity in history. They constantly overlap so that theory must incorporate practice and practice must incorporate theory. By means of critical theory one frees oneself from previous practice and pushes toward new liberating experience. In critical praxis one follows a theory and through new experiences evaluates and possibly transforms it.

Political hermeneutic is basically a theology for active laypersons, not a specialized theology for priests and pastors, as most theologies up to now have been. Its subject is not the hierarchy but the people of God who live in the world with the poor, the blind, the oppressed, and the apathetic and cry out for liberation.

The Ethics of Hope:
Resistance and Anticipation

The political ethics which results from the Lutheran two kingdoms doctrine is an inherently secular, realistic, and conservative ethics. It wishes to see the present orders of state and society as "God's ordinances" and seeks to exercise love within them. Its aim is the preservation of the world against threatening chaos "until that lovely last day" but not the anticipatory realization of the kingdom of God on earth.

Conversely, the political ethics which follows from Barth's doctrine of the lordship of Christ seeks a way between the strict separation of the world and the kingdom of God. Rather than accepting an easy identification of the world with the kingdom of God, it seeks to relate these two with parables, hints, and signs; these point to the kingdom of God in history.

The political ethics which follows from political theology begins with Barth's emphasis, but goes beyond it. Barth's political parables, images, and analogies in the civil community are answers to the already completed salvation event in Christ and the model of the Christian community. But when one begins with the eschatological Christology presented here and understands history as the history of God's future, then these political parables and social analogies have not only a responsive character turned

108

backward, they possess also simultaneously a character of anticipation which is directed forward. By seeking to correspond to Christ in political and social acts, the congregation simultaneously anticipates the kingdom of God. These anticipations are not yet the kingdom of God itself. But they are real mediations of the kingdom of God within the limited possibilities of history. They are, to speak with Paul, a pledge (*arrabōn*) and the first fruits (*aparchē*) of God's kingdom in the midst of human history.

This ethics, then, is christologically founded, eschatologically oriented, and pneumatologically implemented. This world is no "waiting room for the kingdom of God." Though this world is not yet the kingdom of God itself, it is the battleground and the construction site for the kingdom, which comes on earth from God himself. We can already live now in the Spirit of this kingdom through new obedience and creative discipleship. But as long as the dead are dead and we cannot achieve justice, love remains fragmentary. All its works remain in need of redemption.

Furthermore, Pauline ethics, like the ethics of the whole of early Christianity, is baptismal and eucharistic paranesis. It is thus a sacramental ethics. It is preceded constitutively by the baptismal calling in faith and the eucharistic event of community. When Barth speaks in his ethics of parables, signs, and analogies for the kingdom of God, this is also sacramental language. For the mediation of the future kingdom in history is realized in a Christian sense through the sacraments. Barth's ethics corresponds to his doctrine of baptism. Christian ethics, therefore, also makes the future of the kingdom present in a corresponding way. When ethics is understood in this way, however, it is not sufficient to see in liberating and healing acts simply a parable, only a sign, and only a hint of the freedom and salvation of the kingdom. We must go a step further, then, and discover the unconditioned within the conditioned, the last in the next to last, and the eschatological in the ethical just as we believe that the blood and body of Christ are present in the bread and wine of the Eucharist. Thus, real history becomes the sacrament of Christian ethics. Christian praxis celebrates and completes the presence of God in history.

Thomas Aquinas said that a sacrament is a sign of the remembrance of the suffering and death of Christ (*signum commemorativum passionis et mortis Christi*) and simultaneously an anticipation (*signum prognosticon*) of the future glory and, in the coincidence of both, a present sign of grace (*signum gratiae*). Correspondingly, Christian discipleship makes present the remembrance of the suffering of Christ and hope in his kingdom and demonstrates in the unity of remembrance and hope a present freedom. In following up these hints Christian ethics becomes a messianic ethics.

Human persons are not one-dimensional beings. They always live and suffer simultaneously in many different dimensions. Christian messianic activity, therefore, also cannot proceed one-dimensionally but must develop into a complex, interrelated historical process in the various dimensions of human experience. The fundamental, interrelated dimensions in which messianic activity must take place today can be briefly enumerated here.[12]

1. The struggle for economic justice against the exploitation of some people by other people.

2. The struggle for human rights and freedom against the political oppression of some people by other people.

3. The struggle for human solidarity against the cultural, the racist, and the sexist alienation of people from people.

4. The struggle for ecological peace with nature against the industrial destruction of nature by human beings.

5. The struggle for assurance against apathy in personal life.

These five dimensions hang so closely together that there can be no economic justice without political freedom, no improvement of socioeconomic conditions without overcoming cultural alienation and without personal conversion from apathy to hope. Whoever does not understand salvation in the most comprehensive literal sense and does not strive for a network of saving anticipations over the various fields of devastation does not understand salvation holistically.

Christian messianic ethics celebrates and anticipates the presence of God in history. It wants to practice the unconditioned within the conditioned and the ultimate in the penultimate. In the economic dimension this means that God is present in bread and as bread, in healing, as health. In the political dimension God is present as the dignity and freedom of the human being; in the cultural dimension, as solidarity. In the ecological area, God is present as peace with nature; in the personal area we experience God in certainty of the heart. Every form of his presence is veiled and sacramental; it is not yet a presence face-to-face. God's presence encounters human persons in the concrete form of their liberation from hunger, oppression, alienation, enmity, and despair. These forms of God's presence, however, point at the same time beyond themselves to a greater presence, and finally to that present in which "God will be all in all." On the basis of these historical incarnations and indwellings of God it can be said: *"Deus semper major."*

God's real presence as bread, as freedom, as community, as peace, and as certainty thus have the character of an explosive, transcending present. To act ethically in a Christian sense means to participate in God's history in the midst of our own history, to integrate ourselves into the comprehensive process of God's liberation of the world, and to discover our own role in this according to our own calling and abilities. A messianically oriented ethics makes people into co-operators for the kingdom of God. It assumes that the kingdom of God is already here in concrete, if hidden, form. Christian ethics integrates suffering and ailing people into God's history with this world; it is fulfilled by the hope of the completion of God's history in the world by God himself.

Christian ethics makes everyday life into a feast of God's rule, just as Jesus did. The messianic feast becomes everyday life.[13] It wants nothing other than the worship of God in the everyday life of the world (Rom. 12:1).

NOTES

1. Johannes B. Metz, *Theology of the World,* trans. William Glen-Doepel (New York: Herder and Herder, 1969); Jürgen Moltmann, "The Cross and Civil Religion," in *Religion and Political Society* (New York: Harper & Row, 1974), 14–47; J. M. Lochman, *Perspektiven politischer Theologie* (Zürich, 1971); Dorothee Soelle, *Political Theology,* trans. John Shelly (Philadelphia: Fortress Press, 1974).

2. Cf. Fr. Oudenrijn, *Kritische Theologie als Kritik der Theologie* (Mainz, 1972).

3. Metz, *Theology of the World,* 88ff.

4. Jürgen Moltmann, *Theology of Hope,* trans. James Leitch (New York: Harper and Row, 1967). For this, Metz, *Theology of the World,* 115: "Every eschatological theology, therefore, must become a political theology, that is, a (socio)-critical theology."

5. For the theme of eschatological Christology see Jürgen Moltmann, *The Crucified God,* trans. R. A. Wilson and John Bowden (New York: Harper and Row, 1974), 98ff.

6. Cf. to this Wolfhart Pannenberg, *Jesus: God and Man,* trans. Lewis L. Wilkins and Duane Priebe (Philadelphia: Westminster Press, 1968). In his emphasis on the anticipatory character of the message and the resurrection of Jesus from the dead, however, Pannenberg has neglected the contradictory character of this message and of the cross of Jesus. There follows from this a tendency to an undialectical Christology and a conservative ethics.

7. Hans Küng, *The Church,* trans. Ray and Rosaleen Ockenden (London: Burns and Oates, 1967), 64: "The 'lordship of God' is for Jesus not . . . an earthly-national and religious-political theocracy. It is rather a purely religious lordship" (translation altered).

8. Metz, *Theology of the World,* 113.

9. Ernst Käsemann, *Exegetische Versuche und Besinnungen,* vol. 2 (Göttingen, 1964), 105.

10. Jürgen Moltmann, "Toward a Political Hermeneutic of the Gospel," in *Religion, Revolution, and the Future,* trans. M. Douglas Meeks (New York: Charles Scribner's Sons, 1969); Wolfhart Pannenberg, "Hermeneutic and Universal History," in *Basic Questions in Theology,* vol. 1, trans. George H. Kehm (Philadelphia: Fortress Press, 1970), 96–136. See also Jürgen Moltmann, "What is 'New' in Christianity: The Category *Novum* in Christian Theology," in *Religion, Revolution, and the Future,* 3–18; Wolfhart Pannenberg, "Der Gott der Hoffnung," in *Ernst Bloch zu ehren* (Frankfurt, 1965), 209ff.

11. Gustavo Gutiérrez, *A Theology of Liberation,* trans. Caridad Inda and John Eagleson (Maryknoll, N.Y.: Orbis Books, 1973), 15.

12. I have developed this in more detail in *The Crucified God,* 317–38.

13. For the relationship of fest and liberation, ethics and esthetics see Jürgen Moltmann, "Das befreiende Fest," *Concilium* 10 (1974): 118–24.

7

Discipleship of Christ in an Age of Nuclear War

Responsible support of the world orders *of* economics, society, culture, and politics or consistent, undivided discipleship of Christ *in* economic, social, cultural, and political conditions? This is the question today in view of the growing number of nuclear plants, further economic growth at the cost of poor peoples, and the preparation for nuclear warfare. Should we boycott nuclear energy? Must we come up with alternative economic systems? Should we "live without armaments"? Can we afford to buy "no products of apartheid"? Or is it the case that we may not and cannot "drop out" and must therefore exist responsibly with nuclear energy, live with the bomb, and use our economic relationships with South Africa to improve the conditions of the blacks there? Where are the limits of responsible Christian political engagement?

Christian Responsibility for the World or Discipleship of Christ? Reformation Reflections

Responsible participation or undivided discipleship? That was the question which stood behind the consequential and controversial Article 16 of the Augsburg Confession. Unfortunately, it is not clearly recognizable and is therefore overlooked by many that the Lutheran church on *this* question took an unambiguous but also *one-sided* position. The reason was that with this confession at

113

the Augsburg Reichstag the Protestants wanted to enter into discussion with the emperor and Rome, but not with the "left wing of the Reformation," which was at that time still a widespread Anabaptist movement prepared for peace. Together with the Catholic church, the Protestants united themselves in a common condemnation and persecution of the Anabaptists. Who were the Anabaptists and what did they teach?

Article 16 of the Augsburg Confession is an answer to Article 6 of the Schleitheim Articles of 1527 (the Brotherly Union), which Michael Sattler drafted for the first Anabaptist synod. Within a year (four months, actually) Sattler was burned at the stake in nearby Rottenburg-am-Neckar. We begin with a systematic comparison of these two articles.

1. *"The sword is a divine order outside of the perfection of the Christ"* (Schleitheim Article 6).

This sentence summarizes the lived witness of the Anabaptists. The perfection of Christ can only be lived in the consistent and *undivided discipleship of Jesus*. This means that a Christian cannot serve two lords. If a person confesses "Christ alone" as his or her Lord, then he or she must live solely according to the wisdom of Christ as it is expressed for the life of discipleship in the Sermon on the Mount. A Christian is not a person with a divided conscience. Therefore a Christian cannot commit an act of violence, not even to impede or punish others doing violent acts. It follows that a Christian cannot accept and practice a calling in economics and politics; this would compromise his or her faith by forcing him or her to use violence. For the Anabaptists of that time this meant no participation in public affairs which necessitated the use of the sword; hence this meant refusal to participate in the army, serve in the police functions, or hold positions in the court and the state.

The perfection of Christ can only be lived in the *voluntary community of brothers and sisters*. The voluntary community which is constituted by faith, discipleship, and baptism is the true, visible body of Christ. In this visible community of believers there is only admonishment—no force, only forgiveness; no judgment, only love; no calculation, only obedience. This voluntary community which is constituted by faith, discipleship, and baptism is the true, visible body of Christ. This voluntary community of Christ is the visible alternative to the society of laws and compulsions: "It shall not be so among you . . ." (Matt. 20:26ff.). Many Anabaptists demonstrated this alternative in their own life communities: the Hutterite Brothers from Mähren created the *Brüderhöfe*, which still exist in the United States and Canada. The Mennonites founded their own village communities in Russia, Paraguay, and the United States. The current movement of basic communities and alternative rural communities to the land has Anabaptist origins.

The perfection of Christ is proven through the refusal of participation in state acts of violence. The Christian's ministry of peace demands the consistent *defenselessness* of life. The Anabaptists did not believe with Luther that executioners and soldiers could be in a "holy station." They refused participation in such public offices which "necessarily force one to sin." They refused to take oaths and repudiated that private ownership of land and tools which made other human beings into slaves.

Finally, the perfection of Christ can be witnessed in this violent world only through fundamental readiness and willingness for suffering and defenseless martyrdom. Patience, tolerance, and "forbearance" were considered signs of the true church. Indeed, the Anabaptists are the martyrs of Reformation times— persecuted, condemned, and executed by Protestants and Catholics alike. The *Book of Martyrs* and the moving Anabaptist song of 1527—"How precious is the consecrated death . . ."—speak a most impressive language. When Michael Sattler was interrogated at Rottenburg about how to defend against the danger of the Turks stirring out of the East, he replied, "Live defenseless!"

Love of neighbor, defenselessness, readiness for suffering are for the Anabaptist the signs of discipleship of Christ based on personal faith and one's own decision. Is this responsible Christian existence? There remain open questions. The community of Christ and this world stand in exclusive opposition. Only in apocalyptic times has the Christian community experienced such alternatives. From this perspective the community of Christ must separate itself from this world. Is this world thus lost? Is this world, despite its violence and inhumanity, not God's good creation? If the community of Christ separates itself from society, does it not then show only its own "great refusal," not the criticism of this violent world in light of the judgment and kingdom of God?

2. *"All established rule and laws were instituted and ordained by God . . ."* (Augsburg Confession, Article 16).

This sentence appropriately summarizes the witness of the "Lutheran responsibility for the world." If all established rule is *from God,* then the participation of Christians in ruling offices and their conduct according to public laws cannot as such be considered sinful. To civil offices and to actions according to public laws also belongs the Christian's right to "render decisions and pass sentence according to imperial and other existing laws, punish evil doers with the sword, engage in just wars, serve as soldiers, buy and sell, take required oaths, possess property, be married, and the like." None of this contradicts the gospel because the gospel teaches an "eternal righteousness in the heart." The perfection of Christ is not external, but rather internal. It is the "proper fear of God and real faith in God." Because "the gospel does not teach an outward and temporal but an inward and eternal mode of existence and the righteousness of the heart," it does not overturn the worldly regiment but requires that the political and economic orders be kept as "true orders of God" (*conservare tamquam ordinationes Dei*) and that love be practiced *in* these orders. Thus Christians are obliged to be subject to civil authority and obey its commands and laws. Fortunately, the Augsburg Confession also added a phrase at the end of this wholesale declaration of civil authorities, namely, "except when they command to sin" (*nisi cum jubent peccare*). "When commands of the civil authority cannot be obeyed without sin, we must obey God rather than men," says Article 16.

We have here in classical form the basic ideas of Christian responsibility for the world: Every political power contains an element of "good order" without which there can be no common human life. Civil authority is created by God and equipped with a monopoly of force so that social peace might be preserved and political justice established. It belongs to Christians as such to respect and responsibly maintain civil authority. The political obligation of Christians is not the great refusal but responsible cooperation.

But according to which criteria should Christians cooperate? The gospel offers no new perspectives for the transformation of structures but rather only obligates Christians to "love *in* structures." Love penetrates all political and economic orders but does not transform them. It presupposes that in the normal situation God speaks through the gospel internally in the heart with the same language with which the authorities created and set in place by God speak eternally. In cases of doubt, one must obey God more than human beings, that is, the gospel more than the authorities.

But if Christian world responsibility means leading a responsible life *in* the world orders, then this means that God, not the human being, is responsible for it. Christian responsibility for the world thereby gains a fundamentally preserving tendency: against the temptation to disintegrate (*dissipare*) political and economic orders, it conserves them by explaining them as "God's orders." This conservative orientation is grounded in the faith that the preservation of the world by the divinely ordained authorities is willed by God until the end of time (*conservatio mundi*). The criteria for Christian responsibility for the world are thus love and reason. There is no such thing as a peculiarly Christian view of justice or a wisdom which is specifically Christian. This formulation of Christian responsibility for the world makes the Christian unrecognizable in worldly callings and positions, for in ordinary situations he or she chooses to do exactly the same thing that non-Christians do.

The critical questions which arise here are numerous: If the gospel really teaches only the righteousness of the heart, then the thought of the actually lived, incarnated—that is, also political and economic—discipleship is sacrificed. A faith which is made so internal delivers over the external world to other powers which it must then explain as divine orders; these then must be obeyed, but "without sin." But can just any group—militaristic and even terrorist perhaps—who come to power by the use of arms be regarded as a divine order? Should the text be understood to say "all authorities," or only legitimate governments, *legitimas ordinationes*, as the Latin text says?

So just as the Anabaptists stand in danger of pulling themselves back out of the world quietistically and without criticism, so the Lutherans stand in danger of going along with the world as it is and cooperating without criticism. The "silent ones in the land" and the "pious state underlings" thus in the end have little to contribute to peace and justice in economics and politics in the world.

Further, this conflict of the Lutherans and the Anabaptists over responsible participation or undivided discipleship provides no direct way to address the problems of Christian witness in the nuclear age. However, for Christians today the patterns of both of these decisions are always close at hand. These great alternatives constantly obtrude in many individual decisions; the basic thinking for these decisions remains similar to that of the sixteenth century.

"Just Nuclear War" or "Refusal of Nuclear Weapons"?

We begin with the major pronouncements of the Reformed Church of the Netherlands (1962, 1978), of the Protestant Church in Germany (1969, 1981) and of the Reformed Alliance in Germany (1982). According to these pronouncements we must assume that *peace* is the order and promise of God: God wants to live with human beings in a kingdom of peace. Because of this the people of God are given their *task of peace*. Peace means not only the absence of war but also the overcoming of suffering, anxiety, threat, injustice, and oppression. Peace is the blessed, affirmed, good, splendid life with God, with human beings and with nature: *shalom*. It is the commission of Christians to serve this peace in all dimensions of life, to promote it and protect it, but in particular to resist war, the most dangerous form of the lack of peace. Christian churches have always viewed their position against war as only one part of their comprehensive ministry of peace.

In view of the fact and possibility of war there have been among Christians two different approaches:

Principled pacifism (the traditional peace churches). This approach refuses every act of violence, including those acts of violence by which violence is to be prevented. Here the discipleship of Christ is given priority over political responsibility for one's own people. The responsibility for the consequences of this discipleship is given over to God: "Do not have anxiety. . . ."

The doctrine of "just war." Whoever is not a pacifist always explains himself or herself with a kind of doctrine of just war. This doctrine does not intend to provide a justification for war— we must be clear about this—but seeks to apply the moral criteria of justice and injustice to the conduct of war. With this doctrine the moral norms of good and evil are applied to the execution of war. According to this theory, war must be conceived as a means of politics or a continuation of politics by other means. Yet we should be aware of the fact that the doctrine of the just war was not developed for the justification of war but for the limitation of war because no one is allowed to participate in an unjust war. (Both the Vietnam War and the Falklands War, for example, were according to this tradition unjust wars because war was never declared.)

The decisive elements of the doctrine of the just war are:

1. War must be declared by a legitimate authority; it must serve the common good of the state.

2. It must be conducted with a good intention.

3. It must be conducted with the expectation of a good outcome; the general situation after the war must be better than the situation before it.

4. All peaceful means for a resolution of the conflict must have been exhausted.

5. The means of the war may not be worse than the evil which is supposed to be overcome by it, that is, the means must stand in the right proportion to the end.

6. There must be a distinction between soldiers and citizens. The civilian population must be protected.

Points 1 to 4 relate to *jus ad bellum* (the right to war), point 6 to *jus in bello* (justice in war), and point 5 relates to both. Those who

119

find these considerations somewhat macabre in the world today may apply these points to a doctrine of the "just liberation struggle" and think, for example, about the struggle of the Sandinistas against Somoza in Nicaragua. But we in the Federal Republic of Germany and the United States have to come to grips with the possession of nuclear weapons, and now quite specifically the refusal of armament or disarmament; we must in this situation live out our service of peace as Christians and churches of Christ. Our efforts to find the right way have taken place within the context of five related considerations, in the church and in the world generally:

The Doctrine of the "Just Nuclear War." According to this doctrine nuclear war is not to be directly justified but rather confined to prescribed limits. The possession of weapons is not refused. Having weapons is part of the present deterrent system which secures peace. The use of the weapons is subjected to the norm of the appropriateness of the means and the norm of the differentiation between military and civilian population. This means that the massive destruction of large cities is not allowed; only the selective use on military objectives is allowed. The strategy of "massive retaliation," therefore, is not to be justified.

As a result of the strategic attacks on military installations, however, civilian population will be destroyed, and this is inevitable. This inevitability is thus a part of the deterrence strategy because it provides an additional threat to the opponent. But mass destruction cannot be espoused. Hence it is prohibited to be the first to use nuclear weapons. If this is prohibited, then it is also prohibited to prepare for a first-strike capacity. These considerations, arising from the application of the just war theory, do not exclude, however—to this point in the discussion—nuclear armament as such.

By its further development of nuclear weapons, the government of the United States (and the USSR as well) is obviously following the position of just nuclear war: the neutron bomb, the Pershing II, and the Cruise missiles can be employed with precision against military objectives without causing massive destruction of civilian population. Out of the old strategy of massive destruction has developed the more finely tuned strategy of "limited nuclear war." Nuclear weapons are thus *made useable.* Accordingly, the process of increasing armaments is organized more and more. With this increase, however, the threshold of the beginning of a nuclear war has come considerably nearer. And because no one knows whether a limited nuclear war can be kept within limits, the situation in Europe has become not more secure but less secure. As far as I am aware, no one in our European churches is a proponent of a just nuclear war, because the limiting of such a war cannot be assured.

The Doctrine of "Just Nuclear Armament." While the doctrine of the just nuclear war has been refused, the doctrine of just nuclear armament is nevertheless maintained in both pronouncements of the Protestant Church in Germany (EKD) of which we have spoken (1969, 1981): By means of the parity of armaments the present "peace" is preserved; only a situation of parity will allow negotiations for disarmament; and, further, the mutually incredible horror of attack prevents a nuclear war. Because disarmament steps can be taken only on the basis of military parity, armaments must be increased. But this can be justified only if the "breathing space" or "grace period" is used to move from armed peace to a security system without nuclear weapons and to build an international order of peace.

According to this doctrine, therefore, only the *possession* and *threat,* but not the *use* of nuclear weapons, may be allowed. If, however, one is not ready to use what one possesses, no deterrence results. To this extent there is an illusion here. On the other hand, it was already recognized in the 1969 pronouncement: "The expectations which in the early 1960s were connected with international politics on the basis of 'armament control' can no longer be maintained." The breathing space or grace period was not used for peace—not because of bad will but because the possibility did not actually exist. In the midst of the armaments race one can hardly speak of disarmament. The speed of increased armaments is always many times greater than the speed of disarmament talks. (Compare, for example, the relationship between the Geneva talks to limit intermediate-range missiles and the concurrent development of plans for space-war missiles!)

The Apocalyptic Threshold. Among many people today the impression is growing that increased armaments of nuclear weapons do not secure peace but rather lead more deeply into a collective insanity. The deterrent systems have their own laws. Within their logic it is not asked whether something serves peace and life but whether it increases the enemy's fear of one's own strike capacity. Kurt Biedenkopf is right when he calls peace based on nuclear deterrence an "ultimate threshold," because nuclear deterrence presents the threat of the enemy as world destruction. A securing of peace by means of threatening world destruction can never be stabilized as a permanent condition. This situation is therefore unsuitable as the foundation of a permanent order of peace. That an apocalyptic peace of deterrence is not even "capable of gaining democratic consensus" shows that among the peoples of the world there is still a healthy human understanding.

There is ethically no conceivable justification of a possible destruction of humanity and of life on earth in order to protect the rights and freedom in one of the social systems in which human beings live today. A "peace" which is bought with the threat of world destruction is no peace. The peace of deterrence through mutual fear may technically be nonemployment of weapons, but it is not peace. Mutual deterrence through fear is a condition of extreme lack of peace, because it increases potential realities of violence. Even without nuclear war the stockpiling of armaments already destroys the life of human beings and the natural environment. The "military-industrial complex" spreads itself like a cancerous growth and infects all dimensions of life. Unnoticed, a total mobilization has come into being.

We call, therefore, for withdrawal from the apocalyptic threshold, a gradual nuclear disengagement as a first step and then the gradual dismantling of conventional armaments. But is such a withdrawal still at all possible? Does not the turning back from an apocalyptic death zone unto life mean a comprehensive transformation of the whole system in which we live? If for a moment we imagine that the nuclear threat does not exist, we would then have to disband the military, dismantle the armaments industry, establish the state economy without a military budget, free our souls from anxiety and aggression, and. . . . But because this idea sounds so utopian, it is clear that we have never thought it through seriously; this fact shows that we quite pessimistically believe that the "point of no return" has already been reached and that we have become prisoners of the deterrence system. In terms of political rhetoric the "force of the issue" and the "momentum" have already taken the place of free, responsible decisions.

"To Live without Armaments." A person who recognizes that mutual deterrence through fear is based not on a parity of armaments but on an armaments race which is already bleeding the nations to death and can lead to no good end stands before the decision either to go along or to protest. It is therefore understandable that the old movement which worked under the slogan "Ban the Bomb," a "struggle against nuclear death," is being resurrected in Europe today under the self-obligating formulation "life without armaments" (*Ohne Rüstung Leben*). The logic is clear: The use of nuclear weapons is irresponsible and sin.

But if the use is irresponsible and sin, then the possession also cannot be considered responsible, for possession binds the possessor to rearmament, counter-armament, modernization, proliferation, and the like—and also, in the long run, to their use. If, however, possession is not to be considered responsible, then one must withdraw from the universal arms race and devote all of one's efforts to an alternative ministry of peace just as the Anabaptists and Mennonites, who were prepared for peace, have done for a long time.

To live without armaments can have two dimensions—personal and political.

First, Christians who place the discipleship of Christ over responsibility for the world can deny themselves without making their own denial a model and a law for all human beings, Christians and non-Christians. That was the way of the Anabaptists: Defenselessness, bound up with the readiness for suffering and martyrdom, is the way of faith, and this faith is not everyone's "thing" (we can expect it from those who believe, but not from those who do not have the strength of faith; it is a personal commitment, but not a political proposal).

Second, Christians and non-Christians who want to end the arms race can deny themselves and seek to make their readiness to live without armaments a political injunction for all human beings of their nation.

In the first case the risk is personal; in the second case it is also political. In the first case one takes the consequences upon oneself; in the second case one must think of the consequences for others.

Wherein does the risk lie in the second case? Whoever disarms unilaterally and brings to the enemy preliminary achievements for peace can, of course, by this very action provoke the foe to aggression. (For instance, it is sometimes said that England's and France's peace initiatives in 1939 provoked Hitler's aggression.) Even if no aggression results, one can thereby become subject to blackmailing and extortion through the threats of the adversary. In this way one delivers oneself and one's own to the more powerful foe.

Therefore, whoever believes that nuclear war can be prevented only through unilateral disarmament must be ready to sacrifice not only himself or herself but also his or her own people. Such a person must risk the freedom, the rights, and the security of his or her own country in order to save the whole of life on this earth from nuclear death. Therefore, a more conservative group in the European church says that the slogan "live without armaments" serves not the resistance but the intensification of military practices in world politics (*Sicherung des Friedens*, 1980, Thesis 9). To be sure, this risk is not yet provable because as of yet no one has done the experiment, but it is a fear which cannot easily be laid to rest as long as the adversary is believed to be capable, not of the rational, but only of the worst. And this leads to the controversy over what we, the West, can expect of the Russians—the rational or the worst?

"Complementarity." In and of themselves the two basic decisions, just nuclear armament and refusal of nuclear weapons, contradict each other. The EKD pronouncements (1969, 1981), however, recommend a third, combined standpoint. It is the thesis of the complementarity of both decisions which, just as much as they mutually exclude each other, also limit, and in view of the common goal of peace, even complete each other. Out of this idea, then, has been developed the formula of "service of peace with and without weapons." The service of peace without weapons is not seen as alternative service but as directed toward the "goal of international solidarity." It should be possible for an individual to engage in the "service of peace without weapons" in place of his military service "but without thereby forcing him to a decision of conscience against military service," says the pronouncement of 1969. If the service of peace without weapons did not exist, then the armament would become total and without limits. If the service of peace with weapons did not exist, then the service of peace without weapons would be overcome by the weapons of the foe. This complementarity is illuminating, however, only so long as military armament has the goal of preventing nuclear warfare in order to gain time for building another system of peace. But that is an illusion. The complementarity thesis does not remove the personal decisions of any Christian, for no one can decide complementarily. This is a position of church leaders who believe that they must always stand for everyone. But it cannot be the position of Christian persons who must decide this way or that.

Remembering the Sermon on the Mount

Up to now both sides of this issue have made their calculations as if neither Christ nor the Sermon on the Mount had existed. With Christ, however, there comes into the calculation a factor which suspends the whole process and changes everything: It is the *reality of God* which actually supports us all.

"You are children of your Father in heaven," says Jesus. This remembrance calls us out of the conflict. Whoever engages in a struggle and arbitrates a conflict stands under the law of retaliation. Otherwise the parity in the conflict cannot be maintained:

eye for an eye, tooth for a tooth, armament—counter-armament, proliferation—counter-proliferation. When we engage an enemy on the basis of the law of retaliation, however, we enter into a vicious circle from which we can no longer escape. We become enemy to our enemy and horrified by our own fear. We threaten what threatens us and we hate what hates us. We are more and more determined by the enemy. When evil is retaliated with evil, there arises one evil after another, and that condition is deadly. We can be freed from such vicious circles only when our orientation to the foe ceases and another position becomes more important to us.

The love which Jesus puts in place of retaliation is the love of the enemy. Love of friends, mutual love, is nothing special; it is only retaliation of good for good. Love of the enemy, however, is not recompensing but is rather an anticipating, intelligent, and creative love. Whoever repays evil with good must be really free and strong. Love for the enemy does not mean surrendering to the enemy, submission to the enemy's will. Rather, such a person is no longer in the stance of reacting to the enemy, but seeks to create something new, a new situation for the enemy and for himself or herself. Such a person follows his or her own intention and no longer allows the law of actions to be prescribed by the foe. Jesus did not die with a curse upon his enemies but rather with a prayer for them. In his life, his passion, and his dying Jesus revealed the perfection of God: "Be perfect, even as your heavenly Father is perfect."

Of what does God's perfection consist? In no way is a moral perfectionism meant. It consists of that love which is long-suffering, friendly, and patient, which does not add to evil or carry a grudge, which bears all things, believes all things, and hopes all things (1 Corinthians 13). God's perfection lies in the fact that he loves his enemies, blesses them, does good to them, and does not return evil for their evil. It is precisely from this that we all live. The whole world lives from this divine reality, even if it does not know it. As Jesus said, God is like the sun rising on the evil and the good, or like the rain pouring down upon the just and the unjust. Hence, God bears all and maintains all because he hopes for each one. God's perfection is his limitless ability for suffering, his almightiness is his patient suffering for and with all things. God's uniqueness is his inexhaustible creative power of love.

In former times, we have asked only What serves our security, what serves our survival? But now, in listening to the Sermon on the Mount and seeking to experience God's love for the enemy, we must rephrase the basic question: What is the most helpful thing for the enemy? In what way can we best bless those who curse us? How do we do good for those who hate us? To remain concrete for my situation in Germany: Since we Germans fear the Russians (and otherwise almost nothing on the face of the earth), we must ask, What helps the Russian people to gain peace more, our further armament or our disarmament? In what way can we bless the communist who curses us? In what way can we do good for the peoples of the Third World who consider us their exploiter and enemy?

The politics of national security is, to a large degree, a politics of anxiety and fear. Because we have anxiety we demand security. Because we demand security, we increase our armaments. As we increase our arms we give terror to our adversaries. Therefore our adversaries also increase their arms. Quite to the contrary of this system, creative intelligent love arises out of freedom, out of the freedom to be a child of the eternal God (which means out of the freedom from the fear of temporal death). Out of this freedom can come love for the enemy and work for peace.

Can one, however, really become free from this anxiety? One can become at least a bit freer from it when one recognizes the danger and consciously enters into the risk. To the degree that the risk of the vulnerable, defenseless but creative life becomes conscious to us, the more free and patient we become. Only the unknown and the repressed make us really anxious. In this sense I am personally willing and ready to live without armaments.

The Consequence: To Proclaim Peace

I come now to the 1981 Declaration on Peace by the Society of Protestant Theology and the statement of the Reformed Alliance in Germany from August 1982. These two groups have made clear statements against nuclear war and armament, and for disarmament. What follows represents, first, the Declaration of 1981.

Jesus Christ, as he is witnessed to us in the Holy Scriptures and lives among us in the Holy Spirit, is *our peace* (Eph. 2:14). In him the eternal God has reconciled the world with himself (2 Cor. 5:14). Through him the world will be redeemed. Through the gospel he makes his peace to be proclaimed among us (Eph. 6:15).

There are no dimensions of our life in which we cannot be certain of the peace of God. There are no conflicts of our life, neither personal nor political, which are not embraced by God's will for peace with human beings and his whole creation. There are no enemies, neither personal nor political, for whom God's will for peace does not apply.

We deny God's peace when we secure ourselves before our enemies by becoming enemies to them, when we encounter their threat with counter-threat and their terror with horror. God's peace rather makes it possible for us to *love our enemies creatively* by understanding their suffering, by thinking through our own position critically, and by making every conceivable effort to dismantle their and our enmity. Love of the enemy is an expression of the sovereign *freedom of the children of God* and has nothing to do with weakness and submission.

From the modern, military *means of mass destruction* comes not only a *deadly danger* for humanity and all life on earth; it threatens us also with *immeasurable guilt* (and this reflects our experience as German Christians from World War II, after which we must ask how we can come to the judgment of God).

The Reformed Declaration says:

Jesus Christ is our peace. By reconciling the world to God upon his cross he made peace between human beings, God's enemy and God. To him as the risen and ascended Lord belongs all power on heaven and on earth. He has sent his community into the world to witness to his peace, to spread the word of reconciliation and, in obedience to the word, to live in peace. His peace which the world can neither give, secure nor destroy sets us free to pray, to think and to work for peace among human beings. This confession of our faith is incompatible with the opinion that the question of peace on earth among human beings is simply a matter of political calculation and, accordingly, to be settled independently of the challenge and claim of the gospel's embassy for peace. In the face of the threat to peace posed by the means of mass destruction by both conventional weapons of mass destruction and nuclear weapons, we as a church have often kept silent for too long or not witnessed to the will of the Lord with sufficient decision. Now as the possibility of atomic war is becoming a probability, we come to this recognition: The issue of peace is a confessional issue. In our opinion the *status confessionis* is given to it because the attitude taken toward mass destruction has to do with the affirmation or denial of the gospel itself.

It is instructive to compare these statements with the Declaration of the Brethren from 1958:

The deployment of means of mass destruction in the use of the state's threat of power and use of power can only result in the factual denial of God's gracious will for his creation and for human beings. Such conduct simply cannot be represented as Christian. To maintain a position of neutrality on this stance, which is recognized as sinful by us, cannot be harmonized with the confession of Jesus Christ.

What is the significance of these official church statements? What are their convictions? If the use of the means of mass destruction is sin, then the *possession* of the means of mass destruction for the purpose of threatening and deterring the enemy cannot be justified as Christian. Because this threat is effective only if one is also ready to use the weapons, the threat itself is immoral and must also be viewed as *sin*.

The modern military means of mass destruction have changed war so much that the real nature of war is revealed now before everyone's eyes. We have reached the point, therefore, where we must go back and say that all war is irresponsible, is sin, and there can be no justification of it. Every martial threat and positioning which includes the possibility of escalation to universal nuclear war is irresponsible. The current concept "peace through mutual deterrence" is also irresponsible.

The planned *spiraling of nuclear armaments* threatens us all as never before. We therefore demand immediate and binding arms talks among the great powers. We advocate a European disarmament conference with the declared goal of establishing a zone free from the means of mass destruction. We support a gradual disarmament in the area of conventional arms and the agreed-upon building-up of cooperation in Europe and Asia, in particular in the area of economic justice.

The service of peace then must become the content of life in the community of Jesus Christ. Church institutions and organizations can do no other than encourage and help in the formation of this service of peace among Christians. Service of peace which is alive in the congregation and which is being supported by the church leadership should have these three emphases in mind:

1. *Learning love for the enemy.* Wars are spread through *friend-foe thinking.* Through artificially concocted images of the enemy, fears are used and aggressions called forth. Through psychological warfare human beings are led to the disregard for life and are mobilized for killings. The command to love the enemy enables the dissolution of these images of the enemy and of the fears and aggressions which are engendered through them.

If *anxiety before the enemy* is made the counsel of politics, not only external but also internal peace is imperiled. The loyalty of citizens to the government which has been elected by them is then no longer won through fulfilling the mandate to govern but is forced through the spreading of fear, be it fear of enemies of the state or fear of being considered an enemy of the state. The spreading of psychological unrest and public mistrust are the results. Whoever wants, on the contrary, to spread peace will resist the use and engendering of fear in our people. Sober historical and political analyses can also free us in Germany from the fear of Russia and the horror of the communists and make us capable of the necessary concrete political encounter.

2. *Recognizing the real danger and cooperating to overcome it.* While taking up again and intensifying this *East-West conflict,* the great powers have repressed from public awareness the much more dangerous North-South conflict and the danger of ecological catastrophe. The politics of the new armament functions at the expense of help for the Third World and leads to its further exploitation. The poor are already paying for the arming of the rich. Already time, intelligence, and capital are being wasted for instruments of mass destruction and not spent for overcoming hunger in the world. The *Christian's service of peace* in such a

situation must also become the voice and advocate of the silent and dying peoples in the midst of the conflict over spiraling armaments.

3. *Becoming a peace church.* The more the church moves from being a *church bound to the state* to a *free church,* the clearer can become its witness to peace and the less ambiguous its initiative for peace. We believe that the church of Jesus Christ can become a church of peace without sectarian isolation from the world. It will become a peace church to the degree that it confesses *Christ* and Christ alone as its and the whole world's peace and shows the necessary consequences of this confession.

One final remark. I believe that so-called pacifism is no longer an illusion or utopia. Pacifism is the only *realism* of life left to us in this apocalyptic situation of threatened world annihilation. Pacifists are the realists of life, not merely voices of utopia.

PART III

CHRISTIAN CRITICISM OF RELIGION

8

Religion and Culture in Europe

Diversity and Heterogeneity

A European cultural charter must take account of the diversity and heterogeneity of the relationship between religion and culture in the various countries.

It is certainly wrong to harbor romantic ideas of removing all traces of secularization from present-day Europe. The Christian churches in particular seem to find it tempting to link their criticism of the decadence of modern life with a dream of the past as a means of countering the supposed end of modern times with the longed-for Empire of Charlemagne or the Christian West or the House of Habsburg.

But it is also wrong to underestimate the strength and the significance of religion. There can be no talk of religion dying out or of an unreligious age anywhere in Europe. It would appear to be typical of a purely secular view of history to combine belief in progress with an underestimation of the religious yearning of the people and the forces of organized religion. The more the secular belief in progress—be it Marxist, capitalist, or positivist—sinks into the crises it itself creates, the stronger religious passions show themselves, even in public life.

A European cultural charter cannot have as a basis a uniform culture dictated by a single religion nor can it presuppose a culture completely free of any religion. The relationship between religion and culture has become so varied in most European countries that the simple, complacent models of the past no longer meet the needs of present-day reality. They have become illusions of the cultural ideologies.

The predominant religion of the European countries is Christianity. This tells us something not only about Christianity as the dominant religion in Europe but rather much more about what "religion" means in Europe. Christianity is an *eschatological* religion. Like Islam, it has its roots in the messianic idea and passion of Judaism. Judaism, Christianity, and Islam must be seen as future-oriented, hopeful, and therefore constantly aggressive religions. The "kingdom of God on earth," the "theocracy," the "new creation" are the dominating points of reference. The cultures they have determined are thus historically geared to the future and universality. Any comparison with the animistic religions of Africa or the great religions of India and China illustrates the difference between these eschatological and those noneschatological religions. On the one hand, the future course is determined by the balance of forces and the equanimity of the soul and, on the other, by eschatological passion and historical experience.

Since "religion" in Europe is eschatological as a result of Christianity, it has inexhaustible dynamic potential. In fact, the European history of Christianity is a history of constant reforms, reformations, and revolutions of religion and culture, of church and society. Christianity in Europe has evolved in a historical dialectic of controversy, conflict, and divisions in Christianity. During this history Europe has been both unified and diversified. It therefore seems important today to work through the destructive divisions of Christianity on European soil and to liberate them from their separate pasts in creating a common future for the peoples of Europe. A European cultural charter can contribute to the achievement of this goal.

A Longitudinal View

Constantine. The Christian history of Europe begins with the idea of the Constantinian empire. From being a persecuted minority, the Christian church under Emperor Constantine became a *religio licita* and under Theodosius the only authorized *religion of the empire.* The church recognized the supremacy of the emperor over it. The emperor promoted the supremacy of the church in culture and morals. The emperor ensured the confessional unity of the church. The church ensured the religious and moral unity of the empire. This gave rise to the uniform Christian state: one God—one emperor—one faith—one empire. Many Christians saw in this the longed-for kingdom of God on earth. Paganism, Judaism, and heresy were declared crimes against the state in A.D. 380 and were suppressed and persecuted accordingly.

This transformation of the Christian church into a political state religion was, however, accompanied by the emergence of an opposition within the Christian faith—monasticism. Here the old Christianity, prepared for resistance and martyrdom, found a new form of existence. Monasticism safeguarded the Christian identity in the face of its political self-dissolution.

Byzantium-Rome. After the death of Theodosius in 395 the empire split into an Eastern and a Western part, and since that time different courses have been followed. While the uniform Christian state with its idea of harmony of state and church continued in Byzantium for over a thousand years and in Moscow, the "third Rome," until 1917, in the West it fell victim to the invasions of the Teutons as early as the fifth century and gave way to another idea. The political disintegration of the West Roman state produced the not-only-religious authority of the pope (particularly under Leo I, 440–461). The idea of the Christian empire was transferred from the emperor to the pope: It was no longer the emperor who represented the kingdom of God on earth, but the pope. Not the Holy Roman Empire but the universal church was the incarnation of the idea of a Christian empire. After the Cluniac reform the monks became the pope's strongest supporters.

It is not necessary at this juncture to discuss the many conflicts between emperor and pope in the Middle Ages. Of interest in this context is the fact that the state very soon disintegrated into the opposites of the imperial Byzantine church, on the one hand, and papal supremacy, on the other. The first major schism in Christianity and one that has not yet been overcome followed in 1054. Since that time the Western and Eastern churches have shaped the cultural development of Europe in conflicting ways. While the harmony of political and religious power continued even under socialism in the countries influenced by the Orthodox church— Greece, Bulgaria, Romania, and Russia—the conflict between the emperor and the pope became the dominant feature in the countries molded by the Western church. The so-called East-West conflict in present-day Europe partly coincides with the distinction in Christianity between an Eastern and a Western form. The different development of social human rights in the East as opposed to individual human rights in the West also has one of its roots in this first Christian schism.

Rome-Reformation. The next major conflict occurred with the Reformation in Western Christianity. This caused the split in the Western church. The Reformation was certainly intended as a universal reform of the whole Catholic church in line with the gospel and the faith. But the conflicts to which it gave rise resulted in the strengthening of the nation-states and the formation of state churches. Its tangible outcome was the creation of national Protestant churches. The fatality of the religious wars in the sixteenth and seventeenth centuries was avoided only with the help of the sovereign principle *cujus regio—ejus religio*. Thus, the right of the church to political authority was again recognized in the Anglican and Protestant circles. Only with the help of the princes was it possible to resist the Habsburg's universal Catholic monarchy.

On the continent, in Scandinavia, and in the British Isles, the Christian faith and national culture began to come together again. The uniform culture of the Middle Ages was replaced by a multiplicity of national cultures. The gap between North and South to be seen everywhere in Western Europe today has one of its most important roots in this process of Protestant diversification.

This cannot really be called "fragmentation" in the negative sense of the word: The awareness of the unity of the church continued in all the national Protestant churches. And the continuing conflict with Rome and the emperor compelled unity amidst the diversity. In Northern Europe at least, it is inconceivable that the split in the Western church should be overcome by eliminating the national diversity of Christianity. The dream of a uniform Christian West is a lost dream. The only realistic approach is the ecumenical idea of the "reconciled multiplicity" of the European denominations and national churches.

European Humanism. The formation of state and national churches as a solution to the Reformation and Counter-Reformation conflict was possible only in areas with Protestant or Catholic majorities. In countries where the two groups were approximately equal, either one group had to be expelled or exterminated or a completely new approach had to be adopted. Out of the desolation of the religious wars against the Huguenots in France grew that secular enlightenment which sought to resolve the conflict with edicts of tolerance and the right to freedom of religion. In France, the Netherlands, and the British Isles a European humanism emerged which saw itself as the "third power" in the wars of religion, and survived them. The driving force behind this solution was the new urban bourgeoisie. The European bourgeoisie gave birth to a new type of human being, who identified neither with the church nor with the state. Whether Protestant or Catholic, German or Italian, humanity became the task of public and cultural life.

In opposition to the state, which wanted its state religion to hold sway, the individual human right of religious freedom was claimed and won. In opposition to the authority of the churches the individual human right of freedom of conscience was claimed and won. Against the pressure of social homogeneity the right to deviate from the norm and, thus, the protection of minorities were claimed and won.

On the other hand, all that the state needed to do was to find secular legitimation. The churches were forced to respect the dignity of the individual and to relate their truth to the consent of the individual and the consensus of the faithful. Society was opened up to the diversity of human life. Modern Europe and its culture did not, of course, develop along these lines without conflicts or perversions of freedom. But here again there is no going back.

Freedom of religion, faith, and conscience, and the right of the minority are the basic cultural conditions for the existence of Christianity in the world today. Not even the cultural-critical defamation of individualism, pluralism, and permissiveness in modern European society can deny this achievement of European humanism. For only the development of human rights and the establishment of culture and politics on their basis turned the destructive consequences of the split in the Western churches into a positive force. From the division of the Western church emerged an enlightened, humanistic Europe.

State Church—Free Churches. But humanism is not the only solution to the Reformation conflicts in Christianity. It was joined by the establishment of free churches. The humanistic solution is based on the freedom of the individual and defends the individual's freedoms and rights against the great institutions of state and church. This solution remains negatively related to these institutions and relaxes the pressure of tradition only in the individual area. At about the same time, the Puritan Revolution in England produced a different solution to the conflict, one that might be called a necessary and complementary solution: this was the *right of the community,* which was raised up against the state and the state church.

The right of Christians to form independent communities underlies the congregationalist idea. It resulted in the creation of the system of *voluntary religion.* Religion is no longer an institution which one voluntarily decides to join. Religion is no longer a decree of the authorities; it is a community of the people. Applying this principle, the free churches broke away from the state and national churches and won for themselves the right of community at the grassroots level. From this principle the free churches were from the outset supra- and international.

The free churches' understanding of religion has had immense political consequences; the right of the community became the underlying tenet of basic democracy in the Anglo-Saxon world, particularly in North America. The religion of the Republic is the free church, and its basis is congregationalism. Only the United

States has a purely free-church form of Christianity and the corresponding democratic culture. In Britain, the Netherlands, and the Scandinavian countries large free churches developed alongside the state and national churches in the eighteenth and nineteenth centuries.

This further fragmentation of Protestantism can, of course, be criticized. But first the great strength lying in this further differentiation of Reformation Christianity must be recognized. The political and cultural potential released by this differentiation must be recognized. Here again there is no turning back. The way ahead will lead the free churches out of their frequent social isolation into a mutual interest in one another and a common interest in the life of the people and the community of peoples. The ecumenical movement has at this stage developed the idea of the "conciliar community." It respects the uniqueness of the individual and moves him or her out of his or her isolation and into new tasks facing a larger community.

Synchronization and Communication

Having taken a longitudinal section of European church and cultural history, we must now try to examine modern Europe in cross section. There we meet the present of Europe's pasts. As Europe's pasts are full of conflicts and divisions, Europe presents itself in a variety of different traditions.

Europe has many pasts but only one future. Europe can realize the wealth of differences only in view of the past. The only future Europe has is in a new community. For only as a community can Europe become the subject of its own history. But Europe will find its inner unity neither through the hegemony of a single cultural tradition nor by reducing the different cultures to the lowest common denominator. Europe's inner unity will be found only in a community of differences. To reach this end priority must be given to two tasks: (1) *synchronization* of the various extant pasts, and (2) *cultural communication* and overcoming already established identities.

In terms of the history of civilization, Europe is not only geographically an area divided into nations; it is also divided into various periods of history. The Christian reforms and schisms clearly illustrate this: the coexistence of premedieval and medieval, pre-Reformation and Reformation, prerevolutionary and revolutionary forms of life. How can people living at different times as a result of such breaks with tradition discover the community of a single present? This is the task of the synchronization of Europe's different pasts.

Europe has been able to survive its breaks with tradition only by separating the adversaries. This resulted in the separate development of the Eastern and Western churches, of the Roman Catholic and Protestant churches, of the national and free churches. Wherever the *ecumenical movement* endeavors to surmount these divisions, it encounters identity crises which it causes among the Orthodox, Catholics, Protestants, and others. The fear of losing face can be overcome only by offering a greater and better Christian identity in the future. The ecumenical movement lives on the vision of the one, holy Christian church. If the European cultural charter wants to realize the right to cultural communication and the right to cultural identity at the same time, it will encounter similar crises and fears in the cultural sphere. For what kind of future are people and nations prepared to sacrifice a part of the identity they have gained through history? Could this facet of their identity be only that narrow-minded part of their self-validation that is born of fear?

If we look at the relationship between religion and culture in terms of European synchronization and communication, we find not only variety but also certain achievements and developments which cannot simply be ignored. We can synchronize the various traditions only if we take them into these developments and translate them into this new situation. As an indication of the course to be adopted and the tasks that await us, I will begin with the most recent present and end with the most distant past.

1. The separation of the free churches from the Protestant national churches resulted in the right of the community and voluntary membership in a church. This cannot be revoked. It also totally changed the rights and freedoms of the state and national churches. The churches can no longer be servile state churches.

Nor can they continue to exercise authoritarian control. They must be tolerant and, where necessary, prophetic in the cultural life of the people. Where the free churches gain their freedom from the state, the state also gains its freedom from the church. The separation of state and church is a precondition for both developments. The reciprocal delimitation of the rights of the state and of the church is vital to the future of Europe. Neither the state religion nor the religious state is a future alternative for Europe. A European cultural charter must resist the temptation of neoclericalism just as it must resist the dangers of the religious or ideological uniform state, be it determined by Christianity, Islam, or Marxism. But it can do this only if the various Christian churches adjust themselves to a free-church way of life.

2. The religious wars which resulted from the Reformation/ Counter-Reformation division of the churches were overcome on the continent only with the help of the "third powers" of humanism and the Enlightenment. Out of this power emerged the first formulations of *human* rights. The right to freedom of religion, the right to freedom of conscience, and the right of the minority can no longer be abolished. The churches had to accept that humanity had come of age and that people believed not because of an authority's bidding, but because of human judgment. The churches had to accept that the human being was a responsible being who decided in ethical questions according to his or her conscience. A European cultural charter can only allow the churches rights which accord with these fundamental, individual human rights. Europe exists only on the basis of declarations of human rights. The churches in Europe must accept an existence within the framework of these human rights.

3. The difference between Protestantism and Catholicism, which has split the "Christian West" since the Reformation, has an inner and an outer aspect. In its inner aspect, the ecumenical approach has thrived among all people of good will to the extent that one can hardly speak of differences in belief which justify the split. In its outer aspect, however, there still appear to be wide and serious differences in the ecclesio-political conceptions of the mission and authority of the church in society. In practice, the

ecclesiastically interpreted and generally binding moral law and the doctrine of the two kingdoms have little in common. A common basis can be found only when the two ecclesio-political conceptions are today related to the democratic decision-making processes of people and nations. A European cultural charter will, in this respect, help the Catholic and Protestant churches to translate their old ideas into the new situation in which people in Europe live. If they fail to do so, there will be reactions which will split Europe further.

4. The division of Christianity into an Eastern and a Western church is part of European history. It is unfortunately often overlooked. But Europe simply cannot be united according to the idea of a Christian West, because the "Christian East" would then be left out. The Orthodox churches have been members of the Ecumenical Council of Churches for many years. The Christian churches of the West cannot, therefore, be content with any conception of Europe, be it political or cultural, which excludes those Orthodox churches and the people of Southern and Eastern Europe. A European cultural charter must be formulated in such a way that it is open to the peoples and cultures marked by the Eastern church. Since the early Middle Ages, Europe has, sadly, all too often been regarded and unified in terms of the Western church. This unfortunate approach is no longer an alternative. The World Council of Churches and the European Conference of Churches also present the tradition of the Eastern church for the Europe of the future. There can be no Europe exclusively composed of the Western church.

5. Behind this division into an Eastern and Western church there is another division in contemporary Europe—or at least on its periphery. Here the great alternative to Christianity presents itself. This is Islam, which is manifesting itself in Turkey, among some of the Balkan peoples, and among many migrant workers in Europe today. Since the Crusades and the wars against the Moors and the Turks, Europe has often been united in the fight against Islam. In a Europe of the future, however, this conflict must also be resolved. In other words, Europe cannot be unified by Christian ideas alone. Islam joins Christianity as another great "es-

chatological religion.'' How can the often deadly rivalry of the two religions in the past be overcome? Do Christianity and Islam have anything in common?

6. And if we take the presence of Islam in modern Europe seriously and expect a future to overcome this conflict in history as well, then a last step becomes inevitable: *Christianity* and *Islam* have their common roots in the *Judaism* of ancient times. Both have derived the visions and strengths of their hopes from the Bible. Israel, the church, Islam—each has in its own way filled peoples with the messianic spirit. Therefore, Europe's most important religious root is thus to be found nowhere else than in the tradition and existence of Judaism. Christian Europe and modern Europe are inconceivable without the Jews. For the Christian churches in Europe this means concentrating again on the dialogue with Judaism in their own ecumenical efforts and in the religious debate with Islam. For a European cultural charter this means regarding the unique tradition and particular existence of Judaism as a root and a continuing force of the European spirit. Can this mean that the European community must maintain relations of a special nature with the nation of Israel at political levels as well?

Today Europeans may no longer be able to say as hopefully as Lessing did two hundred years ago:

> Are we our people? What then does 'people' mean? Are Christian and Jew more Christian and Jew than human beings? Oh, if only I had found one more among you for whom it was enough to be called a human being!

But whether we are Christians, Muslims, or Jews, the task remains to be human and to achieve what is human. The hope for the human world of human beings emerges from Europe. It is therefore Europe's hope.

9

America as Dream

The American Passion

Much has been written about the political ideology of the United States. How much of the biblical—particularly the Old Testament—symbology dominates this political ideology is a matter that has also been extensively investigated. That the political power of biblical faith experiences and hopes remains unbroken by the secularization process was proved again in the 1976 and 1980 campaigns. Neither the Democrats nor the Republicans could avoid the religious archetypes of the people. Here much more was at stake than *Realpolitik*. In order to acknowledge the campaigns' promises in the face of the underestimated passion of the people, even hard-boiled bureaucrats in Washington had to become soft. Thus, for non-Americans to understand the political ideas of the United States, it is all the more important to grasp why they are collectively called "the American dream" and to recognize their religious roots in the Judeo-Christian tradition of biblical hopes.

For Europeans there exists a simple beginning point for understanding the American dream: before there was an *American dream* there was *America as dream*. But America as dream was dreamed in Europe. It was and is the dream of freedom for every human being: the land of unlimited possibilities and of justice without privileges. This was the dream of the politically oppressed, the religiously persecuted, the socially humiliated and racially defamed. America as dream was also, to be sure, wanderlust, gold fever, and Karl May romanticism. But it was in every case a European dream which motivated the emigration.

The American dream is basically nothing other than the transferal of the European dream of America to American soil. It is the fulfillment and disappointment, the continuation and the reshaping of the European dream of America. Consequently, the American dream did not represent a hope limited to America but had universal significance for all people who sought America as the fulfillment of the hope for freedom and justice. For this reason, on the other hand, an international discussion of the American dream is not an illegitimate meddling of foreigners in the internal affairs of the United States. Yet precisely at this point there lies already the first ambivalence of the American dream: the ambiguity between universalism and particularism, between messianism and Americanism.

The nation entered world history two hundred years ago with all of the passions of political messianism. It lives from the power of the vision to be "a new nation conceived in liberty" (Abraham Lincoln).

It was not poetry but pure realism which motivated Roosevelt to say in 1933: "Where there is no vision, the people perish." With this observation the New Deal program began. Because there was no tradition or common past which united them, a multitude of immigrants, slaves, and oppressed minorities in an unlimited, even if certainly not uninhabited, continent could only find social community and the unity of the state in the future-oriented religion of political messianism. Without the will for a common future this nation would certainly have been destroyed and even today would no doubt disintegrate. Without hope in community, the American identity would dissolve into its old ethnic identities. The Vietnam War led to dangerous internal disintegrations. Thus, almost every president begins his administration with a confirmation of the messianic ideals of the political religion of this people.

In this relatively short history the American people has experienced both the good fortune and the misery of political messianism. Through its dream it became united, active, and successful as no other people. But it has also suffered from its dream because the promise which is deeply embedded in it can neither be fulfilled nor discarded. The ambivalences which are found in the American dream also become plain when it conflicts with American reality.

The dream of freedom, equality, and happiness for all human beings—"We hold these truths to be self-evident: that all men are created equal, that they are endowed by their Creator with certain inalienable rights, that among these are life, liberty and the pursuit of happiness"—is a *human* dream. It can only be fulfilled by humanity as a whole. As long as human beings are alienated from each other by class, caste, race, and nation; as long as they live against each other and not for each other, this dream cannot be fulfilled.

Nor can it be fulfilled as an *American dream;* for as a nation, a world power, and a culture, America must take part in the alienation, separation, and oppression of human beings. The human dream cannot be Americanized without being falsified through the ideological self-justification of the American empire and the free enterprise of the multinational corporations. As a human dream, the American dream is a true and necessary one. As an American dream, however, it makes the human dream impossible.

Basically, involved here is a contradiction which is similar to that of Soviet ideology: The "establishment of socialism in one country" destroys through race identification the socialism of humanity. "Socialism" is falsified through the self-justifying terms of Russian hegemony. If the United States understands itself as "this nation under God" (Abraham Lincoln) or as the "champion of democracy," then ambiguities inevitably arise. Was the Vietnam War really executed for the freedom of the Vietnamese people or for the United States' own interests? At the time, one could hear both claims. The humanization of the American dream would make the United States a blessing for other peoples. But the Americanization of the human dream also makes the United States a burden for other peoples. Thus, the test question for the United States foreign policy is, Will the "moral conscience" be realized in the demand for liberation and the respect for human rights in Latin America, Asia, and Africa, or will the interests of American big business be further served through the ideology of national security (through the National Security Council) at the cost of other peoples?

America as Promise:
Paradise or Doomsday?

White Americans are an immigrant people. Voluntarily or involuntarily they left their homeland in Europe and followed a promise. What they left behind, they cast away as the hopeless Old World. What they sought, they greeted as the hopeful New World. What they all carried with them, however, was no new idea nor different system but simply the promise of open space. It promised to each the unlimited possibilities for the fulfillment of his or her wishes. "Freedom in space," as Sydney Mead calls it, was the clarion call of America.

Whatever else the American dream may be, at its core it is directed toward superabundance: unlimited possibilities, unlimited freedoms, unlimited powers. Of course, nothing on earth is without limits, but there are always new fronts on which one can glimpse the boundless sea of possibilities. The first "front" of the American dream was the open space which stretched westwardly across the continent. For one hundred years the call to go West was the call to freedom, that is, freedom in space. The second front of the American dream was the natural resources and power which became available for technology. The ability to fulfill almost all desires through technical fabrication was, for another one hundred years, the call to freedom, that is, the freedom of power. And now, as one can hear in California, the third front of the American dream is opening in the unlimited possibilities of the soul. The discovery of unused human potential has inspired the human potential movement and the personal growth movement. On all three fronts America does not awaken any new hopes, but it promises the fulfillment of all existing hopes.

"All things possible"—that is the American promise. It is an ambiguous promise so long as human beings are ambiguous creatures who not only have life wishes but also death wishes. This can be rather clearly recognized in the two faces of American eschatology.

No other country on earth—with the possible exception of Russia—has so intensively disseminated *messianic eschatology* as the United States. It has done this theology in its churches and synagogues as well as through political ideology in public acts. By *messianism* we mean here a future hope which is combined with faith in its own realizability on earth. This messianism was fermenting in the Great Awakening, the democratic movement, the Social Gospel movement, and the Civil Rights movement. It also lies at the heart of normal American pragmatism: "If it can't be done, it's not worth thinking about." Americans thus transform every hope into a *program,* every opinion into a *message,* every task into a *mission,* every struggle for the good into a *crusade,* and every new experience into a *resurrection.* Religion exists, therefore, to be realized. This is its meaning.

But no other country on earth has at the same time so penetratingly disseminated *apocalyptic eschatology.* The United States has done this through theology in hundreds of sects as well as through doomsday prophets in best sellers. By apocalyptic we mean here a future anxiety which is combined with faith in the realizability of its worst fears. This apocalyptic ferments generally in fundamentalism and particularly in those missionary groups and crusaders which, for a hundred years, have made the world unsafe. But it is also to be found in the ideology of national security with which the world is plunged into permanent civil war. In Europe both forms of eschatology are perceived to be typically American. Are they alternatives, or do they both live out of the same basis?

At first glance the two eschatologies have nothing to do with each other. Messianic eschatology sounds *optimistic.* Hope is to be fulfilled not only after this age, but immediately, here and now. There is a life before death? Today is the day of salvation! Therefore, I want my freedom—now! This hope is fulfilled by God, by "God with us," and then also by one "nation under God." The truly pious will not be denied by God.

It is the conviction of messianic eschatology that the time of fulfillment is already beginning as never before, and that it is beginning with us as with no others in the world. Messianism in

America is constantly combined with millennialism. Where else and among whom else should the "thousand-year reign"—in which Christ and the heavenly beings are to reign over the devil and all enemies—be inaugurated? If the time of fulfillment is beginning, then what is impossible for other human beings is now made possible.

This optimism is a dream from which one must be awakened in order to become historically conscious and shrewd. Even "with God" the human being is no guiltless creature. In open space the human being fulfills not only his or her best hopes but also his or her worst impulses. In order to awake from the dreams of collective guilt, a nation should know that this is even more the case under God. The phrase "All things are possible" in itself means only the frenzy of power. Unfortunately, the open space and the unlimited possibilities say absolutely nothing about whether this spatial, technical, and spiritual power is used for fulfilling or destroying human life. But if one is to be awakened from the dream of individual guilt and leave the collective delirium behind, then one must hold all the more firmly to the messianic dream. How otherwise could one resist destruction and will life against the threats of death? What else besides this dream of "life, freedom, and happiness" can give ambiguous human beings orientation and courage for life, freedom, and happiness?

On the contrary, apocalyptic eschatology sounds *pessimistic*. It is fear, not hope. Negative experiences of the present are gathered, bewailed, and hysterically escalated until one recognizes in them the threatening presentiments of the global end of the world. Time has become short here. The end of the world is coming, not after this time, but already in it. There is death before life! Today can be the day of calamity. Therefore, save yourself, whoever can! But can one save oneself when the doomsday is assured and already coming? There is scarcely an apocalyptic terror of the soul without a spark of hope: "a remnant is converted" and saved. It is to build the kingdom of the good world after the destruction of the evil world.

Just as messianic eschatology anticipates the kingdom of God in democracy and salvation in the earthly happiness of the greatest possible number of human beings, apocalyptic eschatology anticipates the judgment of God in the total criticism of the present. It anticipates the eschatological separation of the sheep and goats in the decision for Christ against the antichrists. It anticipates hell in the destruction of the world. Whoever is declared the phantom of the "antichrists," whether it be the Catholics, the liberals, the socialists, or the communists, is always the current enemy of religion, the state, or the class. In former times natural catastrophes such as earthquakes, pestilence, and starvation were made into signs of the end in order to engender a belief marked by apocalyptic anxiety. Now unpleasant political events are used for that purpose. Liberation movements in Africa, socialist movements in Asia, but also the destruction of democracy in Chile and South Korea or the undesirable conclusion of the Vietnam War fill the role quite nicely. The apocalyptists become dangerous because they support the very powers that cause these signs.

From where do these two faces of American eschatology come? *Messianic eschatology* stems from the Exodus story of the Old Testament. The Exodus from slavery in Egypt into the freedom of the promised land was the root experience of Israel. The memory of liberation also ruled the hope of the prophets in the new messianic exodus. The Puritan Pilgrim fathers experienced and interpreted as an exodus their emigration from European oppressions into the freedom of the American wilderness. Untold numbers who came after them entered into and experienced emigration according to this archetype. The exodus motif was universalized by the Pilgrim fathers. Since then, it has become the motif of wandering and mobility. From the Pilgrim fathers it was transferred to the advancing pioneer frontier in the West and to the liberation struggle of the black slaves. From both, it came into the Women's Liberation Movement. Out of the ideology of the United States, it is today wandering into Latin American liberation theology. This modern history of traditions framed into the exodus motif is going far beyond Christianity. Traces of it are also found in Maoism. If it is correct that the paganization of the exodus motif and its general politicizing stem from the Puritan

153

Revolution in England, then there lies hidden in the modern spreading of this motif a certain "Americanization" of the world.

Apocalyptic eschatology can also essentially be traced back to the exodus of the Old Testament. Pharaoh and his army had to be destroyed so that Israel could be free. The destruction of the antidivine powers also belongs to Israel's root experience. The apocalyptists projected this experience into the future. The future, ultimate exodus struggle is the final struggle of God against his enemies. This struggle can come to an end only with the victory of good and defeat of evil. In apocalypticism the Pharaoh of history becomes the antichrist, the beast from the abyss, the whore Babylon. The world becomes the great battlefield of God on which Michael and his angels struggle against the dragon and its seed. The saints are the soldiers of God. They are engaged in permanent war and crusade against evil. Out of such apocalyptic representations of the end struggle, without which there is to be no exodus into freedom, is born the idea of total warfare. The end struggle can be concluded only with complete conversion or the complete destruction of all evil. Parallel to this is the method of psychological combat against the internal enemy.

The exodus motif and the end-struggle motif have a common root in Old Testament memory and expectations. Today, however, they appear, especially in the United States, principally in opposition to one another. In the church the anticommunist apocalyptists stand over against the liberal improvers of the world, while in politics the civil war ideology of national security stands over against the civil rights ideology of the liberation of the people in politics.

Theologically, this ambivalence of the American dream can be dissolved only if messianism and apocalypticism are resolutely Christianized. The question of the costs of the liberation of the people remains open in the Old Testament: Must Pharaoh, alien peoples, or part of Israel be sacrificed, or does the God who liberates take upon himself the suffering which is necessary? For Christians only the recognition of the suffering of God in the cross of Christ makes eschatology unambiguous and hopeful. Without voluntary suffering for others, no power becomes the authority of life. Without readiness for sacrifice, America remains an ambiguous promise.

America as Covenant:
Blessing or Curse?

America's political contribution to world history is rightly regarded as *democracy.* The United States has twice entered world wars "to make the world safe for democracy." Democracy means the rule of the people as opposed to a state of ruling authorities; the state of law as opposed to the state of power. It is a political system in which power cannot be used without a common agreement of law. Truth, not the authority of rule, shall make the laws. But these agreements of law by which the use of political power is limited and controlled go back to the religious idea of the covenant.

In his book *The New England Mind,* Perry Miller shows that this nation was created out of the covenant which its citizens formed with God and one another. *America as covenant* arose politically, namely, out of the free and voluntary union of its citizens through the practice of justice and the preservation of their freedom. The United States is the "covenanted nation." Not political power but rather the Constitution according to which the country must direct itself, has authority. The covenant is sacred, because contracts must be kept for the sake of the honor and credibility of the partners: *Pacta sunt servanda.* Accordingly, morality becomes the foundation of politics.

The political idea of the covenant has a theological prehistory in the Calvinist tradition. Beginning with Calvin and John Knox and continuing with Olevian, Cocceius, Althusius, and Hugo Grotius, the human relationship to God as well as to society was repeatedly understood not as pure rule but as a covenant based on mutual freedom. This was so because the Calvinist fathers had in mind a *twofold covenant* established on the Old Testament model: God makes the *first covenant* with the people whom he elects and whom he has freed from slavery. This religious covenant is at once the constitution of the common life and the guarantee of the covenant partners' rights of freedom. The *second cove-*

nant is the contract of rule. In the presence of God the people make this covenant with their king (or the government). The covenant of rule thus presupposes the covenant of the people and can be made only within its boundaries. If a ruler breaks the contract of rule or if a contract of rule is executed which is in opposition to the covenant of the people with God, the offender must be removed in the name of God. This form of constitutional democracy emerged out of the conceptuality of the religious covenant. It remains vital only so long as the people and the individual citizens lay claim in a crisis to their right to resistance and, for the sake of their conscience (as in the case of Daniel Ellsberg), hold fast to the truth that "rebellion to tyrants is obedience to God."

The democratic covenant realizes and preserves freedom. Political power is not a natural event to which one is simply subjected as to the sun and rain (cf. Melanchthon in the Apology of the Augsburg Confession), but rather a moral task of the whole community. To many Europeans, who for centuries have been used to the arrogance of power, the moral claims of American politics seem dishonest and mendacious. Yet it is better to have politics with a bad conscience than politics without any conscience at all!

American democracy arose along with the American free churches. It can evidently be taken over by other peoples only if at the same time the concept of voluntary religion is legalized. State and national churches nowhere create a climate which is friendly to democracy—quite the opposite. The presuppositions for free churches are two in number: (1) Personal freedom of choice and personal responsibility. Those whose religion is predefined for them through tradition, family, and state do not learn this freedom. (2) The right to the formation of the congregation through voluntary union. Those whose church is rigidly ordered by infant baptism, residential district, and state do not experience the free zone of community. Democracy presupposes citizens who have come of age not only morally but also religiously. The free state, that is, the democratic state of law, demands a free church, that is, a voluntary congregation of the people of God. Conversely, a free church demands a free state.

But freedom of choice presupposes real liberation precisely in that area in which choice is to be encountered as received responsibility. Here lies the unsolved problem of political democracy.

For Israel, the covenant with God and with one another became possible only on the basis of the experienced liberation from slavery. Exodus precedes covenant.

The famous covenant sermon which John Winthrop preached in 1630 before landing in the New World concludes with the summons of Moses: "I have set before you life and death, blessing and curse; therefore choose life, that you and your descendants may live." The freedom for this decision of the covenant had brought forth the exodus from Europe.

The enlightened fathers of the American Constitution began with the concept that all human beings are by nature free. They did not take into consideration the factual slavery of blacks, Indians, the poor, and women. Rather, they presupposed an abstract freedom to which, of course, only a small elite could actually lay claim. In this assumption lies not only the danger of ideological camouflaging of real conditions but also an excessive demand on human beings. If human beings who are enslaved in the economic, social, political, or religious dimensions are confronted with the covenant-call to decision, "Choose life or death, blessing or curse," then the covenant will become a curse for them and lead them to death, for they are not able to choose in freedom. It is simply not possible to maintain America as covenant on the basis of an imagined equality of human beings and an abstract freedom of choice imputed to all.

History gives ample proof: "The covenant is broken." Very little of the religious idea of the covenant is left over in the democratic consciousness. What remains leads the shadow existence of what we call today civil religion. Without inner renewal the democratic institutions of the covenant remain empty and are quickly filled up with the bureaucrats of administration who take over decision-making from the citizens and rob them of freedom. The external covenant of democracy requires and yearns for a renewal of the internal covenant, that is, the "religion of freedom."

Thus it is becoming all the more clear that America as covenant cannot continue to exist without *America as exodus*. Only liberated people can be a "land of the free." But only oppressed and restless human beings are interested in liberation and exodus from slavery. America can expect its renewal as covenant and democracy from them: from blacks, Indians, the poor, women, for they still have their exodus in freedom before them. Only economic and social liberation will fill political democracy with new power. Insofar as the "American revolution" proceeds on this way, it repeats and fulfills nothing other than the promise with which it first set out.

America as Experiment: Success or Catastrophe?

For many people throughout the world America represents the *great experiment*. Through their traditions of thousands of years most of the other nations understand themselves as a piece of nature. Culture and nature have become a unity. Every present is burdened with the past. Everywhere one sees the remnants of past times. Next to one of these nations America appears as an artifact. In a very short time after its independence the United States was constructed out of the will and the reason of immigrants. One needs only to compare an American city with a European city in order to observe that *city* is no translation of *polis*, *citta*, or *Stadt*, but designates a new phenomenon. One needs only to compare the farmland in the Middle West with Asian farming villages to see that here also a new relationship with nature has emerged. American cultivation and management of the land is an experiment with the possibilities of space, of which we spoke at the beginning. The city is an experiment with the possibilities of society.

In the land of unknown possibilities one must experiment in order to probe its latent energies and to discover the best possibilities. The experimental life style corresponds to the open environment. It is fascinated by the realm of possibility and is itself fascinating. As Boorstin has said, "America lived with the constant belief that something better might turn up. Americans were glad enough to keep things growing and moving. When before had men got so much faith in the unexpected?" (*Americans: National Experience,* p. 1).

Life as experiment means try it again and again. The future is open, and the future is gracious to the virtuous. Life as experiment means not to accept any piece of reality as final and closed but to go forward in the dynamic of the provisional. Life as experiment is the trial-and-error method. From its very inception America was a great experiment, and up to the present day it understands itself as a great experiment with nature, society, the future, with God. If there is an American life style which is spread throughout the world today, it is this shape of life which is open to the future, enamored of risk, and experimental.

But one must pay a high price for this life as experiment. According to sociological investigations it is the dearest dream of every American to own his or her own house and his or her own land, and on the national average every American moves at least every five years. Forty million Americans per year change their address. As John Steinbeck set out on his *Travels with Charley,* he saw in the eyes of his neighbor something he was to discover everywhere in the nation: "A burning desire to go, to move, to get underway, any place away from here. They spoke quietly of how they wanted to go someday, to move about, free and unanchored, not toward something, but away from something" (p. 10). But to be a person in movement, one must cut off one's roots and live without relationships. The fascinating mobility of the American legs costs the bitter rootlessness of the American soul. Vance Packard has described this *Nation of Strangers* with an abundance of statistics. He found: "While the footlooseness of Americans as pioneers was a source of vitality and charm, several of the new forms that the accelerating rootlessness of Americans is taking should be the cause for alarm." He has thereby overlooked, I suspect, the fact that modern rootlessness is the consequence of the old footlooseness and the necessary price for an experimental life style. As the Great Experiment, America can only be a society of torn roots.

Life as experiment costs not only this price of loneliness in one's own life but also the sacrifice of many other lives. An experiment is only an attempt. One must be able to repeat an experiment. One should, therefore, take into account the failures. One can learn from errors in order to try again from scratch. When one transfers this experimental attitude to real life, one can immediately see its limits. *Medical experiments* on the living, which can lead to life or death and which can leave behind irreparable damage, are morally suspect. It would be better for politicians to abstain from *political experiments*. Was Vietnam merely a *military experiment?* What about the dead then? One cannot experiment with catastrophe.

Making an experiment means leaving everything open and in suspension. But when it comes to a matter of life and death, the point of no return has been reached. Then it is no longer a question of an experiment but an emergency. Death is not an experiment, for one cannot make a new beginning with it. Therefore life is also not an experiment, for it is once for all.

Not to be able to live, to love, and to die with one's whole heart but to be able only to experiment with life, love, and death is the kind of detached life style to which one is forced by the messianism with which America has entered the stage of world history. The messianic *dynamic of the provisional* creates the strength of America, but the *provisional life* is also the weakness of America. To live with a dream and a hope of its realization is something great and extraordinary. But this life in dream is also something very unreal. One lives in the future, inquires about the realm of possibilities, and thereby depreciates what is real and present. The messianic life has both elements in itself. On the one hand, it is able to draw the future into the present and to do already today what will be tomorrow. On the other hand, it can only live in the postponement in which nothing is done in a final way but only in a provisional and experimental way.

To live as a Christian with the American dream can only mean to combine the dynamic of the provisional with the pathos of the final, and in place of the experimental life style, to develop a life style which combines the horizon of hope with the sacrifice of love. Only if one can live, love, and sacrifice life here with one's whole heart does one really trust in the resurrection of the crucified Christ. The hope which is born out of the resurrection of Christ prepares one to live fully in the present and with ultimate love that life which is once for all. To leave life and death in the suspension of the experiment will mean to miss death but also life.

10

Olympism and Religion

The Olympics in Crisis

Today the Olympics are in a deep crisis, and everyone knows it. Does that crisis mean the end of the Olympic games? Has the Olympic idea run aground? In the future will there be no international athletics? Many people in many lands share these concerns and with good reason. I am convinced, however, that every crisis is at the same time an opportunity; every crisis of the old has within it a chance for the new. And if we accept the fact that the old ways have reached a dead end, we must begin anew. Yet a crisis can be resolved only if one goes to its roots and seeks renewal from the ground up. The great and even unique opportunity of the present crisis of the Olympic games, it seems to me, is to reexamine completely the Olympic idea, to understand it better and to implement it more consistently than before.

What is the crisis in which the Olympics are involved? On the surface we find the *political crisis,* which was occasioned by the boycott declarations of the Western nations against the presence of Soviet troops in Afghanistan. Political peace, they say, is the presupposition for holding the Olympic games; therefore, they cannot participate. But when was, is, and ever will this "political peace" be reached in the whole world; and who has the moral right to ascertain this peace and to accuse possible violators of the peace?

Many athletes and athletic organizations see themselves as "innocent victims" of the present crisis that makes impossible their participation in the Olympic games in Moscow. They are right. In athletics there is a dimension of the experience of life and fortune that is not bound up in politics and thus is actually alienated by political interests and considerations. But one must also see that the *Olympic idea* in modern times was from the beginning a *political idea*. From the beginning sports and games represented the Olympic idea not only for its own sake, but also for the benefit of other persons.

Pierre de Coubertin connected two political interests with the Olympic idea:

1. *A domestic political interest.* This interest is "the enormous calming power" of sports for social conflicts. Public sports serve as a "social lightning rod." They become the "connecting link between the different classes." Out of the common jubilation over a winner or a victorious team comes a collective identification. Social differences and conflicts recede behind the spontaneous feeling "We won!" Of course, public sports do not resolve social conflicts, but they do "wipe away" class struggles. They "stabilize" the social order as well as the social disorder. And that, in Coubertin's view, is precisely what they are supposed to accomplish.

2. *A foreign political interest.* This interest is the honor of one's native land. If victories in ancient Olympia symbolized the favor of the gods, then modern Olympic victories are symbols of national glory. "The competitor who takes part in the games thereby lifts up his country and his race" (Coubertin). He is supposed to keep in mind that "his athletic activity is an effort for his country." The superiority of its athletes is supposed to demonstrate publicly the superiority of its own political system, according to socialist sports declarations. "We must regain our Olympic superiority," demanded Robert Kennedy in 1960 for the USA. Athletic triumphs are regarded then as a measure of the international importance of a nation and the productive power of its economic system.

Thus the alienation of athletics from its own characteristic experience of life was, from the beginning, connected with the modern Olympic idea. By linking international sports with national feelings and sensitivities, Coubertin also subjected these sports to nationalistic conflicts. In the meantime (as he could not have foreseen) nationalistic conflicts developed into the international conflicts of capitalism, socialism, and Third World. These conflicts are, therefore, unavoidably also the conflicts of the Olympic games.

If we return to the beginnings of the modern Olympic idea, we must ask critically whether the nationalistic organization of the Olympic games really promotes the sporting nature of athletics or ruins it. If we return to the beginnings of the modern Olympic idea, we must also ask whether the social-psychological function of the Olympic games as sports sensation has not distorted these games into performance contests between professionals in the interest of politics. Are the Olympic games actually still "games"? And if we ask which countries can afford the costs of holding the Olympic games, we find ourselves in the exclusive circle of the rich nations.

Behind the political and economic crisis of the Olympic games, everyone can see clearly the *moral crisis* of today's world. The classical ideals of humanity, which are inseparably connected with the Olympic idea, are disowned as soon as they touch the power interests of large nations. Is this the ancient conflict between high ideals and low political realities? If that were so, then the Olympic idea would simply share the fate of all good ideas. In reality, however, something else is at stake in the present moral crisis of politics: It is a question of short-term and long-term political goals. Short-term are the present political conflicts over Afghanistan and the Western boycott. Long-term, however, is the interest in world peace, which, however difficult it may be, can only be guaranteed by a world community.

The Olympic idea is in reality a part of this necessary idea of the coming world community. If the Olympic games suffer, then the world community, without which we cannot survive, also suffers. If the Olympic idea is dying, that is a sign that our future is dying. In this regard, does it make sense to subordinate the long-term political interest in the future of the world to the short-term interests of individual nations and to renounce one of the few points of contact between people on the path to this world community?

Also in the face of the *moral crisis* of the world, which today has become obvious in the Olympic games, we must return to the origin of the Olympic idea itself if we are to seize the opportunity for renewal. Is the Olympic idea, as it has been continually repeated since Coubertin, capable of showing us a way into the future? Coubertin crowned the modern Olympic idea with his thoughts on the *religio athletae:* a sports religion was supposed to be the people-binding forerunner of a future world religion. In it he saw a "vote of confidence in the future." Today confidence in the future has been perverted into worldwide anxiety. That is the deepest crisis, for the present anxiety kills the future before it is born. Out of what religious sources can the Olympic idea be born again to new power?

The Olympic Religion

For Coubertin, the crowning of the Olympic idea with Olympic religion was necessary because without religion the Olympic idea would lack dynamics, enthusiasm, and the absolute. In antiquity, religion had actually been the driving force in the peaceful competition of athletes. It was the moral court and tribunal for the Olympic festival. The games were a part of Greek religion. Religion came first; the games followed.

In the modern Olympic idea they were reversed: Religion became a part of games. It was "done" because it was needed. Thus the modern *religio athletae* has become nothing more than an artifact.

Coubertin himself was a free thinker and had no desire to become a supporter of religion. Yet in 1894 he called "Olympism" a "two-thousand-year-old idea that moves people today as it did earlier because it meets a need that is among the noblest and most essential to life," "a melody" that resounds again after two thousand years, "a ray of sunshine" that cuts through the fog of the times and, "as the reflection of a joyful hope," lights the threshold of the twentieth century.

From the ancient Olympic religion Coubertin adopted, to be sure, only the useful rituals. The place of the games was to be a "holy area," a "shrine," the entrance of the athletes a "procession," the Olympic committee a "college of priests," the Olympic oath a "ritual of purification," the honoring of the winners a homage by the nations. The games were to be fashioned by many artists into a religious festival. Coubertin declared, "In Olympia they gathered together as a pilgrimage into the past as well as a declaration of confidence in the future. This is just as appropriate for the resurrected Olympiad."

Coubertin also wanted to fill these old and new religious rituals with a common, nation-binding religious élan. By this he meant a spirit that excites, symbolized by the Olympic flame that is lighted. Olympism for him was more than organization. "This is the first and essential mark of the old as well as the new Olympism: to be a religion," he said in 1935.

As the "Ode to Sports" shows, the new Olympic sports are glorified as a "gift of the gods," as "king," as "divine." Since Coubertin adopted from old and new religions of the world only the rituals and feelings but not the gods, then sports themselves—athletes, people, nations, and finally humanity—must become the content of the modern Olympic religion: "Rejoice in the never-ending resurrection of mankind!"

The German *mentor olympicus,* Carl Diem, was a friend of Coubertin's and a true disciple of his religious ideas. In the *religio athletae,* Diem stressed the *humanitas athletae:* For him Olympism is an "idealistic-humanistic favor" that, through the games, is supposed to "take the human race, divided into many religious confessions, and elevate it with a common understanding of pure humanity." The Olympics awaken a true "mood of peace" and make tangible the prospect of a "worldwide brotherhood." Also for Carl Diem, the Olympic celebration meant a "consecration." The Olympic games are the "day of faith in the sacred spring of the peoples."

In 1964, at the opening in Tokyo of the sixty-second session of the International Olympic Committee, Avery Brundage, longtime president of the IOC, made himself the prophet of the new religion. "The Olympic movement is a religion of the twentieth century, a religion with universal claim that unites in itself all the basic values of other religions, a modern, exciting, lively, dynamic religion, attractive to youth; and we of the IOC are its disciples. Here there is no injustice of caste, race, family, money. On the athletic field everyone stands or falls according to his achievement. . . ." Can that claim be demonstrated? Brundage supported his Olympic religious feelings in 1969 with the following statement: "If you remember that into the Olympic stadium of Mexico City marched 114 teams, in which were represented every race, every skin color, every religion, every political viewpoint, including capitalist and socialist, royalist, fascist, and communist, and all marched behind the Olympic flag with the five rings—not because they were forced to, but because they themselves wanted to—then I can assert that nothing like this had ever happened before" (*Der Spiegel,* 52/1969).

Such words of praise for the Olympic religion and sports as world religion are heard again and again all over the world. As yet, they have been neither critically examined nor evaluated. Either this religious side of Coubertin's Olympic idea is taboo in Olympic circles or it is not taken seriously. The present crisis of the Olympic games forces us, however, also to discuss openly this inner religious dimension of the Olympic idea and to consider its weaknesses and its renewal.

Critique and Renewal

The *critique* of the *new Olympic Religion* is not difficult for those theologians and atheists who are schooled in religious criticism. If we read closely the solemn speeches of Coubertin, Diem, and Brundage and if we understand the staging of the Olympic games, we get the impression that Ludwig Feuerbach was the ghostwriter and Karl Marx wrote the screenplay. This modern Olympic religion is actually an idealistic dream factory and an opium for the people. It is a dangerous glorification of spirits, an idolization of the games that robs them of their human quality. Who is served by this elevation of athletic games onto the high and holy level of the religious? Certainly not those who find joy in athletic games. It serves only those who want to exploit athletics for other purposes. Coubertin began not with one of the known world religions, but with religious patriotism in order to move on to religious internationalism. Religious patriotism and religious internationalism are themselves, however, only religious derivatives and dubious substitutes for what the great world religions represent.

Olympism as religion is an idolatry. One can even regard religious Olympism as the classic case of modern, artificially established idol worship. The religious garments of this idol are borrowed from other religions, primarily European. The religious symbols and rituals are not original but adopted secondhand. The Olympic games are no longer held in honor of religion; rather, religion is subjugated in honor of the Olympic games. The religious feelings and energies of the masses are directed toward another object. In the Olympics humanity celebrates itself, worships itself, offers itself, and rewards itself. A religion without God leads to the deification of the human race and its achievement.

At no time nor place is religion only beneficial; always and everywhere it is also dangerous. On that account we must ask the representatives of the modern Olympic religion whether they, with their religious consecration, have not already deprived athletic games of their human element. Certainly one could answer that people need religion. But what remains of a religion when it is used as a means to an end? It suffers the same fate as that of sports when they are used as means for political ends. Such a religion becomes life-threatening, like everything that is degraded and abused.

In spite of this warranted critique of the religion of Olympism, there remains in the Olympic experience and in the Olympic idea something that such a critique cannot destroy but rather seeks to liberate. That something is the true religious dimension of life, which I want to describe in connection with two phenomena.

The first phenomenon is the simple and completely natural human pleasure in sports, the joy in the success of athletic achievement, and the happiness experienced in a well-played game. Sports and games have belonged to the human race for as long as there have been human beings. They are a part of our humanity. In sports people find themselves, discover their strengths, feel their limits. They play with their bodily possibilities and shape their lives. In games they discover their relationships to other people and shape their community. Sports and games have a special significance for the humanizing of human beings.

Athletics have their own worth and meaning in themselves. What is that meaning? In athletics and games one attempts not to make something but to present oneself. Athletes and players are not technicians but artists. They do not produce something that someone can use; they produce something at which one can rejoice. "When man understands himself as free and wishes to use his freedom, then his activity is play," said Jean-Paul Sartre. This dimension of aimless, but, in itself, meaningful play is the true religious dimension in sports. Sports in service of country, sports in honor of socialism, sports as the greatest product of a capitalist, production-oriented society—these are the alienation, abuse, and destruction of the naturally human and thereby truly religious dimension of athletics. Whoever rides a horse should not ride "for Germany" but because he or she likes to ride and rides well. It is necessary and very desirable that the Olympic committee reformulate the *Olympic idea* in order to protect and promote the humanity of sports and the freedom of play.

The other phenomenon that I would like to point out is the hope of freedom that lies in the natural experience of sports and games, and which was also correctly recognized and well-formulated by Coubertin. Every religion is ambivalent: it can be the opium of the people and the ferment of freedom. The critique of the new Olympic religion becomes meaningful when it destroys the opium and brings into prominence the ferment of freedom. The Olympics can be "a declaration of confidence in the future" if the games are no longer set up in such a way that social conflicts are "wiped away" and political disagreements forgotten. The Olympics have within themselves a great potential for protest against the economic exploitation of people, against the racist degradation of human beings, and against the nationalistic separation of one person from another. In Olympic sports and games the athletes themselves already present a world of peaceful competition, mutual recognition, and friendship that offers an alternative to the real world in which we live and suffer.

Are the Olympic games not a prelude of hope to a successful

life for the human race? They are that for all those who can and want to play. The Olympics become the "symbol of hope" when one expounds their character as *protest*, as *alternative*, and as *prelude to freedom* over against the daily life of economics, politics, and society. This is a natural human longing, which has a religious dimension because in it people experience their "ultimate concern" (Paul Tillich). Olympic religion must return to the elementary hope that is inherent in it. It is necessary and very desirable that the Olympic committee protect this hope for freedom against political, social, and economic abuse.

The Olympics as Alternative

The Olympic games have fallen into a crisis today because the modern Olympic idea was, from the beginning, a specific political idea. I see a remedy only if the Olympic idea is taken back again to the original experience of sports and the original hope of the games so that from these sources it can be born again. The Olympic idea cannot be allowed to contain within itself an alienation of sports and an estrangement of the games. The Olympic idea must guarantee protection of the Olympic experience against exploitation by other interests. To that end, the following points seem to me worthy of discussion:

1. The Olympic religion must change from a holy glorification of sports and an impotent dream factory for ideals to a ferment of freedom in this world of hostility and oppression. It must bring the original Olympic experience to critical expression in contrast to other types of experience in life.

2. Public sports, in particular Olympic world sports, are spectator sports. They must no longer be held as substitute for the missing experience of the spectator, but as an incentive toward individual experience.

3. The *nationalistic basis* of modern Olympic games is no longer feasible in an age of political blocs. Participants must no longer be motivated by patriotism, and participation must no longer promote patriotism. Would it not make sense organizationally to tie the Olympic games more closely with the United Nations? Would it not make sense to take the Olympic games back

to Olympia? Would it not make sense to single out and honor the winning athletes, not their countries? The Olympics would become a symbol of hope if they were to become the concern of all the people, not just the concern of the nations and primarily the rich nations.

4. Sports and games are based on a *way of life* and present a characteristic way of life. The modern commercialization of public sports has turned sports into a product, a consumer item, and thus destroyed the characteristic sports way of life. Should not the Olympic idea be able to lead the Olympic games away from this producer-consumer mentality and combine them with a *simple life style* that frees them from a society of production and consumption? The life style of the coming world community can only be the style of a simple and common life. Would it not make sense to lead the Olympic games away from narrow-minded production thinking and the compulsion to consume and to shape them into a new alternative of hope?

Today the Olympic idea is in a crisis. This crisis, however, is the opportunity for its renewal out of the springs of Olympic experience and hope.

11

Messianic Atheism

The Messianic Spirit

Europe has lost, to an alarming extent, its ability to hope for, to wish for, to want great things. The European spirit is like a landscape of burned-out craters covered by a dull layer of lava. Ideologies, utopias, hopeful designs, plans for a better future have become caricatures. A general resignation in the face of the dictatorship of the facts, of the *fait accompli,* rules over the positivism and "realism" of an intelligentsia which only manipulates things on a technical level. Helmut Schelsky once quoted with respect to the intellectual situation of the "skeptical generation" the words of a student: "What all of us under thirty lack is a guiding passion, a moral vision if you will. We are unable to weave a grandiose pattern out of the loose threads of our experience—and we know it." This is not just the sincere feeling of a particular age group; it concerns all of humanity in all areas of knowledge, thought, and action—Christian theology and the church not excepted.

One is tempted to ask where the hope of the kingdom, inspired by the gospel, has gone. Where is the theology based on this hope which is capable of grasping the problems of the world and of history? Is not the institutionalization of the Christian hope, and are not the reduction of apocalyptic to the "eschatological moment" and the defamation of cosmic eschatology as "myth" simply expressions of and justification for a Christian-bourgeois, individualist culture which through existentialist resolution and a situation ethics can be mobilized only insignificantly and subjectively?

173

It is therefore no wonder that the Marxist and Jewish philosopher Ernst Bloch was greeted with so much admiration and applause and was the cause of so much commotion and attention in West Germany when Suhrkamp published his life's work *The Principle of Hope* in 1959, thereby forcing the Aufbau publishing house in East Berlin to bring out there the disturbing, indeed heretical third volume of the work in the German Democratic Republic as well. Bloch reawakened buried, stifled, repressed hopes in both parts of our divided country. He injected a note of uneasiness into both party-line Marxism and the Western consumer world, a note which in its best exemplifications could be described as messianic. His principle of hope may as principle, that is, as an ideology coming out of the school of Hegel and Marx, seem rather conventional; but insofar as beneath this outer garment a messianic passion is hidden, this principle is a challenge to both East and West and, in particular, to Jewish and Christian theology.

One year before Ernst Bloch emigrated from Leipzig to Tübingen I attempted to present *The Principle of Hope* under the title *Messianism and Marxism*. Although it was his humanistic, democratic socialism that in the sixties led students and middle-class people, trade unions and parties, churches and schools to a fundamental reform of life and life's relationships, I was increasingly more fascinated by his messianism. At that time I asked the question: "In Bloch's *Principle of Hope* does messianism win out over Marxism or is it defeated by it?"[1] Today I would not put the question in quite such an either/or way. Messianism seems to me to be the overarching perspective and inner impulse for Bloch's socialism. Democratic socialism is the historical form which messianism must take, given the present poverty of capitalism and its democracies as well as socialism and its dictatorial governments. The messianic spirit shakes both socialism and democracy out of their torpidity and opens both up to broader perspectives. It puts both in a state of suspension, mediating between their hitherto unreconciled opposition and enmity—but only when seen in this suspended state.

In the field of messianism today Judaism, Christianity, and Bloch's philosophy of hope encounter each other. It is a field of surprising variations, of conflicting possibilities. Only in a discussion among Jews, Christians, and socialists can the meaning of *messianism* be more precisely determined.[2] And the moment has come for such a discussion among the different messianic movements, for it is only out of the experience of the messianic *élan vital* and its concrete disappointments that a sober hope which acquires knowledge through experience without discrediting itself is born.

The Messianism of the Founder Religions

In chapter 53 of *The Principle of Hope,* Bloch offers a messianic interpretation of the great religions, especially of the earlier, so-called founder religions. According to Bloch, their special significance lies in the fact that besides the religious mystery and together with it, the "founder's placing of himself into the religious mystery" is also venerated. To the concept of transcendence itself belongs the exceptional human transcending of the world with which every religious act begins. Thus, in the founder religions the unique religious act of the founder is regarded as a first-time event, an example to be exacted and imitated and further to be celebrated as a sacrament of the mediation of the transcendence experienced in it. Of course, the mediator himself is not what he mediates. Yet, because it is only mediated through him, he is seen as "the way." Thus he acquires an intrinsic significance for the goal and a guiding power for all those who search for it.

Bloch speaks in a history-of-religions sense of a "growing" extent to which the founder places himself into the religious mystery. This idea of an evolution in religious development is, admittedly, a construal—a construal based on the religion which advertises itself as the "absolute religion." Bloch takes this claim over from Hegel. If he does not declare Christianity the "absolute religion," as does Hegel, he nevertheless does inquire about the consummation of the history of religion. This yearning after the consummation of the history of religion is messianic. It leads indeed to an absolutization of one's own religious experience and to a relativization of all other experiences, as well as to a relegation of all self-willed, premature consummations to the realm of historical incompleteness.

This ambivalence is easily recognizable in Bloch's presentation. He finds this "placing of oneself into the religious mystery" consummated in Moses and Jesus. Through his religious act Moses made God the "Exodus-light" of his people. Out of the "God over us" comes the "God before us"; out of the high lord of heaven comes the future kingdom of his glory on earth. Through his sacrifice Jesus penetrates the transcendent understood as human tribune and transforms it utopianly into the kingdom.[3] This is all still constructed along the lines of Hegel's "absolute religion" with, to be sure, the difference that for Bloch the history of human consciousness of God in no way counts already as the history of the divine consciousness of itself, but rather only aims at the final exposition of the messianic "hope in totality."

Bloch's key phrase "Where hope is, there is religion" leads to his idea of Christianity as the "essence of religion" to the extent that in Christianity the "human-eschatological, in which a messianism ready to explode is set" finally appears.[5] At the same time the opposite is also valid, "Where hope is, there is atheism," to the extent that in atheism and its criticism of religion is intended this same human-eschatological, in which a messianism ready to explode is set. This is the ambivalent mystery of Bloch's "religion in inheritance," hope in totality, for this "religion in inheritance" can mean an inheritance of dead sayings and in this respect be irreligious, and it can also mean the fulfillment of what is only promised in religion and in so doing be more than religious. Thus Bloch refers to it at one point as "without religion" and two pages before as "not simply no religion."[6] This double meaning is a typical sign of the messianic pathos of the end. It must, in the same breath, terminate and fulfill. Hence, Bloch's atheism must also come out against "God" and for God, if he wants to be consistent and not settle for easy substitutes.

Messianism and Utopias

Toward what is Bloch's messianism aimed? The symbols of the goal that he uses are variable, suspended, unstable, and vague:

"totality," "exploding consummation," *"ens perfectissimum,"* "home of identity," "habitableness in existence," "transfiguration of nature," and over and over again "the kingdom," signified astralmythically (and with Dostoevsky) as "crystal," or seen in a biblical sense as "glory." Over against the laws and customs of this world, these symbols demand a "re-birth," a "leap into the totally other." Bloch likes to speak in these contexts of the "most unconditioned utopia," of the utopia of the absolute, of the not presently existing, the not yet being. It announces itself in various signs and signals but is as such not yet known by anyone. It is mystically experienced in the darkness of the lived moment, but cannot be seen and understood in the as yet unchanged world. This messianism of the *totum*, the kingdom, the glory, or the identity Bloch considers to be "the salt of the earth and also of heaven."[7] The messianism which proclaims such a future in history must make known that this future, even in the best possible society, is unattainable by pressing its thorn in the "unabolished intransigence of the surrounding nature."

As is well known, Bloch dealt extensively with the social utopias of happiness and their realization through scientific socialism and the legal utopias of human dignity, and their political realization through human rights and democracy. But these are for him only partial utopias, utopias taken out of the "*totum* of utopia" and looked at in an isolated, narrow-minded, one-sided way. Outside of the "*totum* of utopia" they lose their context and their best intentions. In this "*totum* of utopia" an absolute is anticipated "wherein still other conflicts besides the social ones are resolved, wherein also the understanding of all former frameworks changes."[8] Bloch thus in no way attempts to reduce the messianic utopia or indeed any religious images of hope to actual, real-world social or political utopias, but rather attempts exactly the opposite, that is, the integration of these partial utopias into the *totum* of utopia. In so doing he is not just a metaphysician, but also a metaethicist, metasocialist, metareligionist.

Whoever—whether out of fear or hope—had assumed that in the "classless society" religion would simply be buried and forgotten will be disappointed by the ending of Bloch's book, *Natural Law and Human Dignity·* "Certainly a no longer antagonistic society would hold all worldly destinies fast in its hand, determining an economic-political conformity. But for just this reason the triviality of existence rises in a much more noticeable way to the surface, from the jaws of death up to the level of boredom, of satiety. The messengers out of the nothingness have lost the simple values they carried in the class society but have a new, still largely unimaginable face, and indeed the series of necessities which they interrupted also consumes again in a new way."[9] Thus Bloch's utopian view of the classless society ends with a vision of a new religion as the "re-connecting of a total dream forward to our needy patchwork"[10] and the vision of a new church which "with friendliness takes the deeply urgent and with brotherhood the difficulties seriously," a catholicity in solidarity, an ecumenical community, "so that it does not live for its time, but over and beyond its time"—a "church without superstition and on its way."[11]

Whoever—again be it out of fear or hope—had assumed that Bloch must stylize Jesus of Nazareth as a social rebel or political revolutionary will be no less disappointed. The idea of the messianic kingdom in the preaching of Jesus did indeed begin as a social movement among the miserable and heavy-laden, the humiliated and wronged because it gave them an impulse, a feeling of dignity, a hope. But in its intended content and scope it in no way coincided with just any social utopia. The liberating gospel for the poor anticipates as historically necessary a form among these invisible people which in itself has yet to appear and which will explode the entire system of heaven and earth according to Revelation, namely, the kingdom.[12]

The absolute, total hope content of messianism is claimed in the symbols of God and the kingdom of God. It stimulates ever new social and political utopias related to specific situations and is the driving force behind liberation movements and people's struggle for justice. Hope itself, however, goes beyond this; it leads people through these utopias and beyond them. It contains a concrete utopia and more than utopia. It is a real revolution and more than revolution. This superabundance of messianic hope becomes, despite the transformations of the God-hypostasis under the eschatological impulse, indeed because of this transformation, that which is no longer itself transformed and which thus again and again transforms even the transformations. Messianism becomes concrete through its production of real utopias and their mediation with the subjectively and objectively possible. It transcends continually into the immanent. But it also continually puts its own realizations into a state of suspension, the suspension of the compelling not-yet, and becomes immanent in the transcendent.

Whoever begins to live messianically comes ever closer but never quite makes it all the way home.

Messianism and Atheism

"Without atheism, there is no place for messianism"—so goes Bloch's thesis.[13] But what in this context do *theism* and *atheism* actually mean? We read: "The existence of God, indeed God in any sense as essence, is superstition."[14] Religion itself is superstition when it is not hope and its symbols are not symbols of that most absolute utopia, inviting one to the moment of hope. Bloch's atheism is decidedly against any hope symbol of the *totum* hypostatized as "God," that is, an entity existing for itself. When God is thought of and worshiped in such an absolute way, then hope is paralyzed. Thus all the representations of God as Creator and Ruler of the world, as heavenly power or enthroned authority fail for Bloch. "God becomes the kingdom of God, and the kingdom of God no longer contains a God, that is, this religious heteronomy and its thing-oriented hypostasis dissolve completely in the theology of the community, but as a theology which itself has crossed over the threshold of the hitherto existing creature and its anthropology and sociology."[15]

As with Feuerbach, so it also goes with Bloch, rather monotonously: God hypotheses are "nothing other than. . . ." Nevertheless, the messianic bond of atheism does not allow religious symbols to be reduced to the level of any anthropology of presently existing humans or the sociology of the present society. "God" and the "kingdom of God" converge on a practical level only in the going beyond of the past and present form of the creature and will finally converge only in the eschatological leap of the "Behold, I make all things new." It is the "religious intent of the kingdom as such with which, in the final analysis, atheism is involved,"[16] and nothing else. If, then, there is no place for messianism apart from atheism, so atheism is also powerless without messianism.

Grasping the messianic intention of atheism and of Bloch's critique of religion is necessary to a correct understanding of his thought. His atheism is not a reductionist atheism, not a simplistic explanation, much less a limitation to the merely banal. And despite the similarities with Feuerbach's thought it is not about some reductionist atheism of the future. As in the best parts of Marx's thought, so it is with Bloch: He is merely concerned with a functional criticism of religion, not with a critique of the essence of the religious. He is simply looking for a new functional interpretation of theism in the light of messianism. Theism is superstition when it causes superstition. And it cannot effect hope until its functions have been interpreted in a new, messianic way. Theism has an alienating, imprisoning effect on people when it puts a religious hold on experience and hinders messianic transcending. If experience, practice, and analysis had shown that belief in God had had a liberating, stimulating, mobilizing effect toward a real transcending of poverty, oppression, and alienation, then this functional criticism would have been unnecessary. The criticism of the old praxis of belief in God can only be overcome through new praxis. This is the level at which Marx's and Bloch's functional criticism of religion operates.

Behind this is another level. It is the impulse behind the *mosaic commandment against graven images* which Bloch, like Adorno before him, applies to the Judaic and Christian religion, to Christian theology, and to the metaphysical "imaging" of reality itself. When the Yahweh religion became too influenced by baal-worship, the Old Testament prophets used the commandment against graven images to sharpen the differences between Yahweh and the baalim. Within the political religions of Christianity, the idolatries of the Christian faith have also been criticized in a similar way by the theology of the cross and the discipleship of the cross.

Bloch's atheism is influenced by this commandment against images, which is radicalized in the Jewish prohibition against speaking the name of God or representing his being, and to a large degree is a carrying out of this commandment. Religious symbols built upon religious experience must not dogmatize this experience, otherwise they harden it, fix it, and thus end the pilgrimage. They ought rather to invite one on to further experiences and discoveries, to the movement of transcending; to do this they must remain open and underway.

Symbols of the origin always guide people back to the same starting point. They form the *restitutio in integrum*. Eschatological symbols, on the other hand, invite people to break away from the same old thing and to a new experience of new life. As signs of the change, they are themselves changeable signs of a journey which does not turn back. In Bloch's symbolism is found his preference for symbols of the *incipit vita nova*. His demythologization for the purpose of the eschatologization of religious symbols has support in the messianic tradition of Judaism; when the messianic era breaks in, the oppressive idols and demons will disappear from the world.[17] The earth will become human and inhabitable. One of the ideas of messianism is that the messianic era will, among other things, fulfill the commandment against graven images worldwide. The messianic era will so transform the world that human understanding will be able to abandon its doubled, alienating world of images.

Behind this level of the commandment against graven images stands then a third—the messianic level. According to cabalistic tradition, the messianic world will be a world without images. In this world the image and the imaged must no longer be somehow related to each other because in it appears a mode of being which no longer needs to be, indeed is not capable of being, imaged.[18] The distance between God and creation, faith and experience, consciousness and being will disappear.

Does not Pauline eschatology also contain this vision? When all dominion has been done away with and death has been destroyed, then God will be "all in all" (1 Cor. 15:28). If, however, God is "all in all," then the distance and difference between God and the world which had to be bridged in history with symbols, images, representations, and hypostases no longer exists. The foreignness of God over against the world and the alienation of human beings from God are abolished in God's glory which lives in all, permeating all. Thus also ended there are all symbols and images of the Other which in history take part in God's foreignness and humanity's alienation because they can point to that home only in an alienated way. They are "the song of the Lord in a foreign land" (Ps. 137:4) sung by the imprisoned people of God. "God all in all" is no longer capable of being imaged, nor is this any longer necessary because he does not need to be represented by anything else or mediated through a third party. This vision is of the immediate nearness of God which makes pictures, symbols, signs, and codes superfluous.

This also applies to theological concepts. That which in history and in alienation is called "God" is grounded in the exodus experiences of history and refers to the glory which will permeate all, but it is itself still part of the foreignness and alienation which must still be overcome. The glory shines forth in a light that up to now has not yet (according to Jewish messianism), or has already (according to the Christian faith in the paradoxical form of the resurrected crucified one) come forth from its source. That which no one has yet to see or hear, which has only made an appearance in the unseemly and unassuming figure of Christ shall in the kingdom transform and transfigure the world. With respect to the historically conditioned alienation of the theisms, the kingdom of God will be "atheistic." Thus, these historically limited theisms can be interpreted messianically, namely, in their making of themselves superfluous in the unmediated presence of God.

Bloch remains messianic insofar as his statements in this area remain equivocal and double-edged. "*God* becomes the *kingdom of God,* and the *kingdom of God* no longer contains *God*"—this thesis is, if not simply frivolous, highly paradoxical in its contradictory use of the word "God." If a simple reduction were implied, then the kingdom ought not to be called the "kingdom of God." If the messianic interpretation is correct, then "God" as an entity existing for itself outside of the world in the coming kingdom becomes the glory indwelling the world. The "kingdom of God," then, really does not any longer contain a "God" existing for itself separated from and outside the world.

The following phrase also contains this paradox: "This religious heteronomy and its thing-oriented hypostasis dissolve completely in the *theology* of the community. . . ." They do not dissolve in the autonomy of humanity but in the "theology of the community." This can only refer to, as the closing phrase about a crossing over of the "threshold of the hitherto existing creature" shows and the similarity to Hegel implies, God's indwelling his people through the power of the Holy Spirit, the "God in us" and "with us." In the Spirit-presence of God and in the new creation in which God fully dwells the religious heteronomies and objectified hypostases are, in fact, dissolved.

The phrase about the "fulfillment of the exodus-God in the kingdom, in the dissolving of Yahweh in this glory"[19] is also to be understood messianically. The exodus-God fulfills himself in the God of the kingdom and this "fulfillment" is, at the same time, the "dissolving" of his historically manifested and historically limited Yahweh-form in the form of that glory of which, according to the vision of the prophet, "the whole earth is full" (Isa. 6:3). Of course, alongside these, one also finds in Bloch many statements which, à la Feuerbach, make it sound as if the mystery of God is "nothing other" than the mystery of humanity.[20] With such statements, however, Bloch falls below the standard of messianic thought and of his own better insights.

The Cost of Messianism

Gershom Scholem, at the end of his tract on "The Messianic Idea in Judaism," named the price which the Jewish people have had to pay and which they continue to pay even today for this idea which they themselves gave to the world. The greatness of the messianic idea directly corresponds to the weakness of the Jewish Diaspora which was not prepared, in exile, to enter into the historical plane because it dreamed of returning home. The messianic hope kept the Jewish people alive during the time they were scattered among other peoples. One lived from year to year with the thought, "next year in Jerusalem." But for just this reason one did not live with a heartfelt commitment in the present. The messianic idea has the weakness of the preliminary and provisional which docs not give of itself, but preserves itself, which cannot die because it refuses to live. "To live in hope is something great, but it is also something highly inauthentic."[21] The messianic idea forced upon Judaism "a *life-in-deferment* in which nothing can be done or executed in a conclusive way."[22]

It was not until after Auschwitz, in its return home to Zion, that Judaism found itself ready to enter irrevocably into the concrete political world—certainly a move accompanied by the messianic overtones of Zionism, but without the commitment to some sort of metahistory. Whether it can maintain this effort without foundering on the rocks of the messianic demand is a life-or-death issue for Israeli Judaism. Jewish messianism becomes concrete in Zionism. But Zionism has also put the messianic hope in a crisis situation, a situation of self-defeating fulfillment, so that either the messianic hope must be reduced to the terms of the Sinai and the Golan or else the transcendent element of messianism must be reborn.[23]

Bloch's philosophical messianism also puts the world in a state of suspension: "Such a conscientiousness . . . mindful of being hope-in-totality comprehends simultaneously the essence of the world in a state of tremendous suspension, towards the Tremendous—a situation which hope believes in, which active hope urges on, as being a good thing."[24] Bloch uses a rich variety of symbols to characterize this state of suspension into which the messianic idea brings the world and the experience of the world, symbols such as "open world-process," "process matter," and *"experimentum mundi."* On the one hand, this sounds encouraging; nothing is conclusive, everything is open, "Poland is not yet lost." Hope can be disappointed—otherwise it would not be hope—but it cannot be destroyed by any disappointment because no disappointment is final. This contains within itself, however, the weakness which Gershom Scholem pointed out—nothing is done in a conclusive way; everything remains preliminary, revocable, provisional. Life in this "suspension," in the "tremendous suspension" of the hope in "the Tremendous," can only be a life of continual deferment. Every word remains open, every thought remains fluid, every act revocable. Everything is only an "experiment." The core of existence cannot be pinned down because it has yet to appear, indeed is truly unable to come out into the open.

But where and in what way does the conclusive, the entering into the concrete without reservation or possibility of evasion, the complete sacrifice, the ability to die come into this continually preliminary because hopeful messianic life and thought? Even when this messianic life in hope is not interpreted negatively as a "life in deferment," but positively as a "life in anticipation," even when life in the dynamic of the preliminary is not defined by the continual "not-yet-real," but rather by the "now-already-possible," this question persists as a criticism of the theory and practice of the hope-principle.

If we attempt to overcome the weakness of messianism and Bloch's principle of hope without destroying them both, then we must introduce the paradoxical elements of the ultimate into the dialectical categories of the preliminary.[25] Otherwise, we can scarcely avoid the danger of considering the world an always possible, but always unreal, world of appearance, and of not living or not yet living or only experimentally living our lives in this world.

Dietrich Bonhoeffer wrote along his road of no return, in his final prison cell and under the influence of his reading of the Old Testament: "It is only when one apprehends the unspeakability of the name of God that one may also speak the name of Jesus Christ; it is only when one so loves life and the earth that with them all seems to have been spent and have come to an end that one may believe in the resurrection of the dead and in a new world."[26] Now, of course, Bonhoeffer earlier in his *Ethics* drew a careful distinction between the "next-to-last" and "the last,"[27] but in the face of death he recognized that both—love and death as well as resurrection and a new world—are "last things." The sacrifice of life in love and the irrevocable entering into the concrete can only be accomplished with the same absolute passion that one has in hoping for the resurrection and the kingdom of God. Sacrifice and hope, death and resurrection do not harmonize with each other in some middle position between death and life, neither in the friendly, undecided world-process nor in a life-in-deferment. Sacrifice and hope can only occur in a final, an ultimate way. They are not brought into any sort of "suspension" without losing the best part of their thrust.

According to Jewish and Christian traditions, the messianic era begins with the death pains of the old and the birth pains of the new world. It began, from a Christian perspective, with Christ's passion and death on the cross. It was not Jesus' placing of himself into a transcendent mystery, "even unto death on the cross," which inaugurated the messianic era and the messianic life. For this reason, hope can only be put into practice through a complete placing of oneself into the concrete world. This is no state of suspension, no open process, no merely experimental mode of conduct but rather the paradox of living and dying in light of the cross and resurrection of the Messiah. There is then no transcending of hope without the paradoxical countermovement of the incarnation of love, no breaking out to new horizons without the sacrifice of life, no anticipating of the future without first investing in it. It is in the incarnational movement even unto passion and death that, paradoxically, the kingdom of God can even now be lived and not just hoped for. The real life of hope in fellowship with the crucified Messiah will not manifest itself in any other way, for "as dying . . . behold we live" (2 Cor. 6:9). Without this paradox of the real, the dialectic of the possible remains unauthentic.

NOTES

1. "Messianismus and Marxismus,"in Jürgen Moltmann, *Gespräch mit Ernst Bloch. Eine theologische Wegbegleitung* (Munich: Chr. Kaiser, 1976), 31.

2. For this see Gershom Scholem, *Die jüdische Mystik in ihren Hauptströmungen,* 1957; *Von der mystischen Gestalt der Gottheit,* 1973; *Judaica,* 1963; Schalom Ben-Chorin, *Die Antwort des Jona,* 1956; *Jüdischer Glaube,* 1975.

3. Ernst Bloch, *Das Prinzip Hoffnung* (Frankfurt am Main: Suhrkamp, 1959), 1402. (Hereafter PH.)

4. PH, 1416.

5. PH, 1404.

6. PH, 1416 and 1414.

7. PH, 1415.

8. PH, 1411.

9. Ernst Bloch, *Naturrecht und menschliche Würde* (Frankfurt am Main: Suhrkamp, 1961), 310f.

10. Ibid., 312.

11. Ibid., 312, 314.

12. PH, 1493ff.

13. PH, 1413.

14. Ibid.

15. PH, 1408.

16. PH, 1415.

17. Ben-Chorin, *Die Antwort des Jona,* 112.

18. Scholem, *Judaica,* 72ff.

19. PH, 1493.

20. Cf., e.g., PH, 1515ff.: "God as utopian hypostacized Ideal of the unknown human being."

21. Scholem, *Judaica,* 73.

22. Ibid., 73ff.

23. Jochana Bloch, "Selbsthauptung. Zionistische Aufsätze," *Zeitstimmung* (61/62, 1972).

24. PH, 1409.

25. Cf. Hermann Deuser, *Sören Kierkegaard. Die paradoxe Dialektik des politischen Christen* (Munich and Mainz: Chr. Kaiser and Matthias-Grünewald, 1974).

26. Dietrich Bonhoeffer, *Widerstand und Ergebung* (1951), 112f.

27. Dietrich Bonhoeffer, *Ethik* (1949), 75ff.

12

Church and Israel: A Common Way of Hope?

Opening of the Dialogue

The formulation of this theme has already given offense: Why not "Church and Synagogue," as these two religious communities name themselves? Why not "Jews and Christians," as in the title of well-known working groups in Germany and the United States? Why not "Christianity and Judaism," if one desires to examine and compare the two different religious cultures?

With the name *Israel,* politics come into the discussion: the politics of the State of Israel, of Zionism, of the PLO, of the Near East, politics of East and West, of oil interests, of security interests, and much more about which the church, in any case, is not competent. For the "church" is a nonpolitical organization; Israel, in contrast, is a state. Thus the theme "Israel and Church" compares what seems incomparable.

Yet these and similar objections can be raised only so long as we Christians, and especially we Christians in the Federal Repub- lic of Germany, unconsciously assume as self-evident that we are the ones who define the Jewish conversation partners and tell them who they are and how they are to understand themselves. If as Christians we begin with a Christian definition of the Jews, we are incapable of dialogue: we have our position already fixed, affirmed, and judged and expect only the affirmation of our preju- dice from the conversation. The Christian definitions of *Jews,* of *Torah Judaism,* of *Talmud Judaism,* of *Synagogue Judaism,* of *post-Israel Judaism,* and so on have been one-sidedly set forth and for the most part used negatively. They were intended to serve not so much the understanding of Jews as the self-understanding of Christians.

A dialogue based on such premises cannot be a genuine dialogue. In the best case it consists of two monologues and in the worst case of an interrogation. Unfortunately, Christian faith conversations—not only with Jews and people of other religions but also among Christians themselves—are often interrogations for the purpose of judging the other. They are not expressions of community, but rather of the acceptance or rejection of the other, of the decision between friend and foe.

In a free and fruitful dialogue each must be able to enter as he or she is and be taken seriously as he or she understands himself or herself. A genuine dialogue begins first, then, when prejudices fall away and preconditions are no longer set forth. That is clearly easier said than done, for when the "image of the enemy" becomes unclear, one's own identity, which is often supported by this image, also becomes uncertain. If the identity of Christians is made uncertain because Christian definitions of the Jews are no longer acceptable, the well-known fears and aggressions will ensue; one must count on that. Thus, the timid beginning of Christian-Jewish dialogue in Germany has been followed by massive negative reaction.

Anxiety about one's own Christian identity, however, is as superfluous in dialogue with Jewish non-Christians as in dialogue with other partners. Whoever is overcome by an anxiety about identity in dialogue apparently has a rigid, unchangeable, schematic, and weak identity; an identity which lives from the denial of others; an identity which reacts aggressively. In truth, one does not lose one's authentic identity in dialogue with others but rather gains a new profile over against the other.

We learn to see ourselves in the mirror of the other and to recognize ourselves in the eyes of the other in a way in which we would otherwise not be able to do. For Christians, and especially Christians in Germany, this is a humbling process, for to recognize ourselves in the eye of a Jew means to be looked upon with the eyes of the victim and of the survivor of Auschwitz. Yet for us it is the only way in truth not only to the recognition of actual history but to authentic Christian existence after Auschwitz. Clearly, one does not invite the victim to "dialogue," as Johann Baptist Metz has correctly pointed out.[1] Yet the hesitancy occasioned by the shame of guilt must not become hesitancy from which the victim suffers. The dialogue which the Jews have begun with us Christians after the Second World War is a precious offer. It is an offer which has again given hope to many of us in the shadow of Auschwitz.

Christians in Germany cannot get around Auschwitz. We cannot limit our concern with Auschwitz to the circle of the executioners in order to distance ourselves from the crime. We will not be able to historicize Auschwitz in order to move ourselves beyond this event. Only together with the victims of Auschwitz and its survivors and their descendants will we come through Auschwitz into another, better future. Only when we can no longer forget Auschwitz will the Jews perhaps be partially unburdened from the constant remembering of Auschwitz.

What one has suffered, one never forgets. What one is guilty of, one represses quickly if one takes it seriously at all. This inclination to irresponsibility makes us blind about ourselves and blinded to our victims. Awakened conscience resists this; it makes the blind see. Authentic Christian faith resists this; it knows that guilt can only be canceled through forgiveness, never through repression. The forgiving of guilt, however, provides an ever-present reminder so that we do not unknowingly repeat it. The forgiving of guilt makes us into neighbors toward those to whom we bear guilt.

With the remembrance of Auschwitz, politics enters into the dialogue between Jews and Christians in Germany, whether desired or not. The recognition of guilt in and acquiescence to the destruction of European Jewry by National Socialism makes up a specific kind of politics. The Stuttgart Confession of Sin of the Evangelical Church in Germany in 1945, in which the destruction of the Jews is unfortunately not clearly named, is related to politics and has itself become political.

Auschwitz was to be the "final solution" of the "Jewish question." The Jewish question, however, existed already for two thousand years inasmuch as Jewish existence was brought into question by the Christian church and the Christian empire. Insofar as Auschwitz is not only a burden of the Christian in Germany but is also the endpoint of a long anti-Jewish development in Christianity, the process of rethinking must therefore not only overcome faithless Christianity, the un-Christian, and the anti-Christian in Germany, but also must lead to a rethinking of Christianity at its very roots. The root of authentic Christianity is Jesus himself.

Through their growing anti-Judaism the Christian churches through the centuries have increasingly paganized themselves. Out of the congregation of "Jews and Gentiles" to which Paul spoke came heathen religious institutions for the satisfaction of the religious needs existing within a people. This transformation of the Christian congregations into the political religion of the nation was a political process.

The nationalization of Christianity and socialization of the church since Emperor Constantine have separated Christians from Jews. If they are to find each other today in a new community on the way, then a critical distancing of Christians from the political and civil religion in which they exist will be required. The dialogue between Christians and Jews lies thematically in the triangle of Israel-church-nations. The more nationalized the church allows itself to become, the further it pulls away from Israel. The more Christians gain a critical distance from the political religion and ideology of the state in which they exist, the more they recognize their community with the Jews.

The Jewish-Christian or Christian-Jewish dialogue was from the beginning a theological-political dialogue. In a symbolic sense it concerns the assessment of the Roman procurator Pontius Pilate and his role in the murder of Jesus. Did Pilate as representative of the Roman Imperium have the Son of man from Nazareth crucified just as he had nailed to the Roman cross so many agitators against the Imperium and its slave system? Did Jesus "suffer under Pontius Pilate" as the Apostles' Creed says? Or did he suffer under the Jews? Did the Jews crucify him, and can Pilate "wash his hands in innocence"? Is Pilate justly considered holy in some Christian churches? In order to fit into and survive in the Roman Imperium, did Christians so transmit the trial of Jesus that Jesus is construed as suffering only under the Jews but not under the bloody and brutal Pilate, as if the stubborn Jews but not the Roman oppressors were guilty of his death? As worshipers of a Jew who was crucified as a "rebel" in Jerusalem by the Roman occupation forces, the Christians in the Roman Empire could not have lasted long. They would have been suspected everywhere as a subversive element, as it in fact actually did happen in the persecutions of Christians. The tendency to accommodation to the Roman Empire is already recognizable in the way the story of Jesus' death was handed down and in the early church's interpretations and preaching.

If, then, dialogue from the side of Christians in Germany after Auschwitz and from the side of Christians everywhere "after Pontius Pilate" cannot be carried on nonpolitically, how much less can one bracket out the political existence of the Jews? In a dialogue without preconditions one cannot require, as was done in the history of Christian nations, that Jews give up their Jewish existence and appear only as persons. One cannot require that they sacrifice their hope in the Messiah in order to represent themselves merely as "adherents to the Mosaic religion," as has been proposed in the past. Likewise it cannot be demanded today that a Jew denounce his or her Israeli citizenship in order to speak exclusively as a representative of "Judaism."

The name *Israel* is in reality a broader, more inclusive name. It embraces the biblical Israel, postbiblical Judaism, the various forms of historical Judaism, and finally the present State of Israel. It is not our concern here to find to whom the promises to Abraham apply, just as it is not the concern of the Jews to find out to which Christian confession the promises of Jesus apply. We have to accept each other as we are and to judge each other according to what we believe. Through our faith we open ourselves to public criticism if our actuality as Christians and Jews is to be measured by our claim of being Christians and Jews.

The founding of the State of Israel is clearly connected with Auschwitz, although Auschwitz was not itself the original cause. Through the founding of the state the relationship between Christians and Jews and between synagogue and church was set on a new level: Jews encounter Christians for the first time in nearly two thousand years no longer "in the Diaspora" but rather "in the homecoming"; no longer only as Jews but also as Israelis. They encounter the church no longer as the religious community of the synagogue but also as the Israeli civil community. That is also for the Jews themselves a new situation which must be grasped not only in practical but also in theological terms. On the one hand, for the first time Jewish existence can again be lived whole, that is, in its own land, with its own people, in its own culture, and according to its own laws. On the other hand, the "whole of Israel" has not yet "come home." The preponderant part of the Jews lives far away in the Diaspora among the nations and as yet has no intention of migrating to Israel, even though the great majority welcomes and supports the State of Israel. It is through the founding of the state that a process of redefining the meaning of *Judaism* has begun. This discussion is not yet closed even in Judaism itself. The political and theological assessment of the State of Israel according to the viewpoint of Judaism is still so open that one should refrain from an assessment from the viewpoint of Christianity. Nonetheless, for the first time in the long history of the Jews, Christians today encounter Jews who are both Jews and Israelis. Therefore, the dialogue from the Jewish side can no longer be purely religious; it must also be political, if it is to be carried on honestly.

Dismantling Christian Judgments and Prejudices

In order to prepare oneself for a dialogue in openness and without preconditions, it is necessary on the Christian side to dismantle those theological prejudices which until now have handicapped and burdened the dialogue. The debris of centuries-old prejudice must be cleared away on both sides so that the exigencies of the present can be accepted and a common future freely perceived. I

194

will limit myself here to short sketches in order to indicate the pattern of those Christian viewpoints which are to be condemned. They have been more fully analyzed by others.[2]

1. *The Viewpoint of Religious Indifference.* From this position, Judaism and paganism are for Christianity the same and of equal worth. As the "religion of salvation," Christianity speaks to all sinful people, whether they be Jew or pagan. The requirements of salvation make them equal before the Savior, regardless of what differences exist between them otherwise. There would be this Christian religion of salvation whether or not there had been an Israel and thus also if there were no more Jews. The existence of Judaism brings nothing essential to the Christian religion of salvation and removes nothing from it. It is not dependent upon Judaism. The religion of salvation has neither more nor less to do with the Jews than with Buddhists or communists.

This standpoint was advanced by the influential Protestant theologian Friedrich Schleiermacher in §12 of *The Christian Faith.* "Christianity does indeed stand in a special historical connexion with Judaism; but as far as concerns its historical existence and its aim, its relations to Judaism and Heathenism are the same." For in view of salvation Judaism has lost its special "promise of the fathers." Regarding redemption, its election means nothing. This viewpoint ruled for a long time in the centers of world Christianity in Rome, in Geneva, and in Constantinople: the "Dialogue with Judaism" was placed in the secretariats and departments for "Dialogue with Non-Christian Religions." It was not carried on in terms of its own theological self-understanding. The designation *non-Christian* was sufficient to characterize Judaism, as if there were not a common writing called by Christians the Scripture, as if Christianity were rooted merely historically, and not also theologically, in Israel's promissory history.

Today an understanding of the special relationship of the church to Israel and of Christians to Jews has prevailed in these secretariats and departments. But even now there are many Christians and Christian theologians for whom Christianity and Judaism are nothing other than two different religions.

2. *The Viewpoint of the Necessary Contrast*. From this viewpoint Christianity arose out of a basic contradiction of Judaism and endures in this antithesis: The Old Testament set forth God's law and its requirements, but the New Testament offers God's gospel and love. "The Jew" appears in the symbolic figure of the Pharisee, but "the Christian" appears in the symbolic figure of the Good Samaritan. Israel retains its special relation to the kingdom of God through its own election, but the universal church gives all human beings an access to the kingdom of God. The ground for these differences and the decisive point is said to be the crucified Christ.

According to Rudolf Bultmann, the history of the Old Covenant is "the history of the failures" of the people of Israel toward God and God's law. It had failed because it did not understand God and God's action in a radically otherworldly way but instead misunderstood it in worldly, historical, and political ways. Israel wanted to become God's "possession," and in this it broke down. It wanted to gain the righteousness of God through the works of the law, and in this it failed. It wanted God to be only for the pious, and because of this it perished. In contrast, Christian faith justifies a person by the grace of God. It sees God "beyond" and leads each individual person to an "otherwordly existence," that is, to an existence which understands itself not in terms of the given, or in terms of belonging to a people, or in terms of one's own works but rather in terms of the transcendent ground of existence. The believer, however, in order to understand himself or herself radically out of the transcendent ground, must constantly dispose of all groundings of existence in this world. Therefore Bultmann said, "Rather does faith, to be sure of itself, require us to know about the significance of the law—otherwise it would constantly be subject to temptation through the law—in any form whatever. In the same way faith requires the backward glance into Old Testament history as a history of failure, and so of promise, in order to know that the situation of justified man arises only on the basis of this miscarriage."[3]

Here the relationship of Israel and church and therewith also the relationship of the Old and New Testaments are expressed in the scheme "Law and Gospel" and forced into the question: "Righteousness through works of the law or through faith alone?" The correctness of this fundamental "question of justification" cannot be disputed, but its application to the relationship of the Old and New Testaments as well as to the relationship of the church and Israel is one-sided and leads to blindness. If, according to Bultmann, faith "demands" knowledge of the law, if the New Testament "demands" the backward glance at the history of Old Testament failure in order to make itself more sure and to "confirm itself," this means for the understanding of the Bible that Christians preserve the Old Testament only as a shocking example and use it for the purpose of its permanent supplanting. For the relationship of the church and Israel, this means that Judaism would survive only as something supplanted and denied by Christianity, that is, as a failed effort. In this view Christian faith is, of course, bound to Jewish existence but only in a negative way, as its opposite: the clearer the Jewish failure through law, the brighter the gospel of the Christians.

In this scheme of law and gospel, Christian faith can only find a negative identity. It is only "sure of itself" because and to the degree that it recognizes the Jewish failure of the law. The justified person can elevate himself or herself only because of this failure. Every identity circumscribed by a negation of the negative remains an aggressive identity: It needs an opposite in order to secure itself. Therefore, this contradiction is carried over to each and every thing. The capacity for differentiation is lost.

The danger of self-righteousness exists in fact everywhere among Jews and also among Christians, and especially among those who can only secure themselves through constant limitation of others. This danger has nothing to do with the real difference between Christianity and Judaism.

3. *The Viewpoint of Inheritance.* From this viewpoint the history of Israel is judged as nothing other than the prehistory of Christianity. The people Israel served as the history of salvation in preparation for the coming of the nations' church. Since Christ

and through Christ, the church has stepped into the place of Israel. Judaism next to it can only be seen as an anachronism. Actually, it should no longer exist.

Paul Althaus advanced this view with clarity: "Israel has a special and unique place in the salvation plan of God; the Church is built on the foundation of the history of God with Israel. The Church is grounded in Israel as the chosen people of God, but Israel speaks also in the Church. The Church is now the people of God, the 'Israel of God' (Gal. 6:16)."[4] From this follows his judgment: "Since Christ, in whom its salvation history calling has been fulfilled, Israel as the historical people no longer has a theological or 'salvation history' significance. In the Church and for the Church, Israel has no more special position and no more special salvation calling."[5] As the fulfillment of all of the true promises of Israel, Christ is also the end of the earthly and temporal promises of Israel. Thus, in a double sense of the word, the church has *supplanted* Israel—preserved and nullified it.

Since God has chosen to carry forward God's plan of salvation through the church of Christ, Israel has stepped back into the rank and file of peoples and is, like all other peoples, the subject of the Christian mission of the gospel. Theologically, since Christ Israel is "disqualified" and "profaned."[6] The Christian faith can allow no "salvation calling" of its own to Israel. The "promises to the fathers" for a people and a land are invalidated through Christ. The Christian faith is interested in neither world nor salvation history. The individual history of the justified sinner, whether Jew or Gentile, comes to the fore. Thus, the Jews no longer have a witness to the name of God and no unique future in the kingdom of God. Their future of salvation is the church. Since Christ there is no longer any difference; all are sinners and will be justified only through faith.

These viewpoints make up the actual triumphalistic view of Christianity. Whether one sees Israel as prehistory, as a first stage, as a salvation-history preparation, or as tentative bearer of promise makes no difference: Israel is superseded by the Christian church. The church has stepped into the "inheritance" of Israel. Yet only the dead or those incapable of reason can be disinherited. The concepts that the church should take the place of Israel, that Christianity has superseded Judaism, and that the Christian faith has taken possession of the promise of the Old Testament covenant function basically on the declaration of the death of Israel, naturally to be understood in a theological sense.

Why should one engage in dialogue with a people whose inheritance one has gained, whom one has dispossessed, disqualified, and profaned? This Christian definition of the Jew must truly be seen as the heaviest burden for the dialogue. It is fully unacceptable for Jews and unbearable for Christians.

This viewpoint has maintained a unique variation through the theological assessment of differences between Israel and the Jews which are in themselves historically right.[7] The Israel of the Old Testament can only be seen as bearer of the promise and as the chosen people. Postbiblical Torah Judaism and Talmud Judaism, it is assumed, are something else. These Jews can only be seen as the successors of the people chosen by God. They are only descendants of Old Testament Israel. As all other persons, they exist in sin, and, as with all others, the promises which are fulfilled in Christ apply to them. Viewed theologically the Israel of God should have existed only until the death of Christ. After that, Israel's most important inheritance, the Hebrew Bible, the Christian Old Testament, is supposed to have passed on to Christians as well as to Jews. This common inheritance binds Jews and Christians, yet its interpretation—with or without Christ—separates them.

Seen ideologically, this salvation-history "inheritance" theology represents the double dispossession of the Jews: (1) They are separated from the promises to their fathers. They do not really belong to Israel but only to its "descendants and successors." (2) In view of the Scripture, they are only co-inheritors with Christians; they inherit as do the Christians from Israel. Therefore, in the dialogue between Christians and Jews there is only a conflict over inheriting the Scriptures. It is conducted through scriptural interpretation.

This Christian absolutism is in reality a Christian poverty: It can demonstrate its faith in the fulfillment of all of Israel's promises in Christ only by declaring the concrete promises—for example, the promise of a nation and the promise of land—to be invalid.

The separation of postbiblical Judaism from the Israel of the promises to the fathers serves only the theological disqualification and the profaning of the Jews. Dispossession from the inheritance is the goal of this terminology differentiating between Israel and the various forms of Judaism. It is not difficult to imagine how Jews could degrade present-day Christians into descendants of the primitive New Testament congregations in order to differentiate between the various forms of historical Christianity so that the present Christian conversation partners could no longer raise a claim to the promises of Christ. Such theories do not serve dialogue; nor do they serve community. Whom, then, do they serve?

4. *Uncertain Identity?* The Christian definitions of Judaism we have sketched do not serve the understanding of Judaism but rather the demarcations of Christianity from Judaism. But do they thereby really serve the self-definition of the Christian? Can Christian self-understanding be strengthened only by fixing the boundaries over against others and through the rejection of Israel? Then the Christian faith would not be a certainty but a weak and uncertain thing. The Christian yes to Jesus the Christ must feel so threatened by the Jewish no that it can only uphold itself through the continual condemnation of the Jewish no. Its proclamation of the unconditional and therefore universal grace of God would stumble over the special promise to Israel. The usual Christian hesitations about a Jewish-Christian dialogue are grounded in the fear of having to give up or relativize "basic Christian truths" which separate Judaism and Christianity.[8] Yet what are these basic truths which separate and do not bind together? How can truths, if they are truly "basic truths," be given up or relativized through a dialogue? Christians must truly be very uncertain of their own truth if they are overcome by such fears.

Behind this, of course, is also a theological problem: Does the universal abolish the particular? Does the eschatological supplant the historical? The Christian objections to Israel enumerated above deny all of the special characteristics of Israel on the basis of the universality of grace; God is gracious to the sinner, whether Jew or Gentile. God justifies the godless and accepts the poor. Therefore, there is no special election of Israel. Paul ended his complicated discussion of Israel in Romans 9 to 11 with the simple yet universal truth, "For God has consigned all men to disobedience, that he may have mercy upon all" (Rom. 11:32). All privileges, prerogatives, and salvation-historical differences seem to collapse before the universal perspective.

Yet does this Christian universalism really replace the uniqueness of Israel? Does this eschatological view repress a regard for the historical way? Are, then, the election and promise of Israel self-righteousness? For the Jewish Christian, Paul clearly not. It is true that there is no difference. "Since all have sinned and fall short of the glory of God, they are justified by his grace as a gift, through the redemption which is in Christ Jesus" (Rom. 3:23, 24). Yet the gospel continues in its historical way "to the Jew first and also to the Greek" (Rom. 1:16). Precisely because God desires to show mercy to all, God holds true to God's promises to Israel and does not cast off God's people (Rom. 9:4f.; 11:2). The universality of grace opened Paul's eyes precisely to the sense of history, for he said of the Jews: "As regards the gospel they are enemies of God, for your sake; but as regards election they are beloved for the sake of their forefathers" (Rom. 11:28).

This is a twofold view of the Jews: one side in light of the gospel, the other side in light of the promises of God. In light of the gospel they are enemies, but "for your sake," that is, through their no comes the yes of God's mercy to the Gentiles. If the whole of Israel would have accepted Jesus as the Messiah, there would have scarcely been the messianic mission to the Gentiles out of which the church developed. It is thus an enmity out of which God has worked good; therefore an enmity "for your sake." Yet, in light of the promises to the fathers, the Jews remain "beloved," for God does not regret God's gifts and callings; God remains faithful to them. The light of the gospel thus does not darken the promise to Israel but puts it much more in its proper perspective. For the messianic gospel is, according to the Jew Paul, the law's fulfillment and end; yet it is also the confirmation and empowerment of the promise.

The Christian universalism of the justification of sinners does not abolish the specialness of Judaism, but rather recognizes and respects it. According to Paul, Christ has done something special in his self-sacrifice for Jew and Gentile. For "Christ became a servant to the circumcised to show God's truthfulness, in order to confirm the promises given to the patriarchs, and in order that the Gentiles might glorify God for his mercy" (Rom. 15:8–9a). The universality of God's grace does not level the theological differences between Israel and the nations, but rather makes the differences much more concrete. Therefore, the Christian polemic against Jewish particularism in the name of Christian universality is groundless and deceptive.

Building a Common Hope

An essentially different, positive estimation of the existence and theological significance of Israel developed first in the Reformed Federal theology of the seventeenth century and later in the nineteenth-century Lutheran theology of salvation history, which was influenced by it. Here Israel's relationship to the church was interpreted not only by the scheme of law and gospel but also by the scheme of promise and fulfillment. In this way the promises of the fathers were taken seriously, not obscured or liquidated by Christianity. Their simple thesis is: Israel has, alongside the church of the nations, an eternal "calling of salvation," for God remains true to God's promises. Less clear and more conflicted was the specific meaning of this "calling of salvation" of Israel next to the calling of the church to salvation. The thesis was grounded on two thoughts.

1. The promises of the Old Testament and the hopes of Israel are fulfilled only *in principle* in Jesus Christ and only *partially* fulfilled through the outpouring of the Holy Spirit in the last times. But if according to the witness of the New Testament they

are only in principle and partially fulfilled, then through Christ by the power of the Holy Spirit the promises of Israel come to all peoples. Through the gospel for all humanity, the promises to Israel are broadened just as it was prophesied of the messianic time. Yet this does not mean that the church can be the fulfillment of the promises of God and the end of Israel's hopes. Rather, Christianity waits next to Israel and hopes with Israel for the future redemption of the world. Christianity is next to and in relationship with Israel, the other community of hope. If Christians confess Jesus as the promised Christ, the Messiah, they must also recognize through his coming, his sacrifice, and his resurrection from the dead the still unfulfilled "surplus" of the promises of the Old Testament in which Israel trusts.[9] It is only the Parousia of Christ which will bring the fulfillment of all promises which are being experienced here in the historical and messianic time only incipiently. Only the coming Christ fulfills the hope of redemption of this as yet unredeemed world. Since Christians are also saved only in this hope (Rom. 8:24), it is impossible for them to take the place of the Jews and repress their hope. The church is not yet the kingdom of God, but it is already the gathering of the people of God out of all nations for this kingdom. In the imperfect church, Christians hope for the perfected kingdom.

If the church grasps its historical provisionality in view of God's redeeming future, then it recognizes Israel as its companion on this way and respects Israel in this hope. The church is Israel's younger sibling in the promissory history of God. And if the church hopes not for its own glorification and triumph but rather for the victory of the righteousness of God and the redemption of the world, then its hope can only be a hope which embraces Israel, not one which excludes Israel. Christians hope in the kingdom of God and therefore have hope for Israel. Their hope is not that Israel will be converted to the church and all Jews become Christians. Not the church but the kingdom of God is Israel's future. Likewise the church cannot hope one day to be converted to Israel so that in the end all Christians become Jews. Not Israel but the messianic kingdom which perfects Israel is the future of the church. At the end is neither a church triumphant nor an Israel triumphant but rather the triumph of the righteousness of God.

2. This alignment of the church with the Parousia of Christ and his coming kingdom is not grounded in every eschatology but only in that eschatology which positively accepts chiliasm.[10] With this view we enter a very controversial area of Christian teaching on hope.

Chiliasm is the teaching of the "thousand-year reign of Christ." The biblical grounds for such a hope are to be found above all in 1 Cor. 15:23–24 where Paul accepts the following resurrection process: "But each in his own order: Christ the first fruits, then at his coming those who belong to Christ. Then comes the end, when he delivers the kingdom to God the Father after destroying every rule and every authority and power;" and in Rev. 20:1–6 where John speaks of the chaining of the devil and of the first resurrection of the martyrs to lordship with Christ for a "thousand years." The hope for a thousand-year kingdom of Christ, in which the martyrs are resurrected and righteousness rules unresisted by evil, is really historical, temporal, "inner worldly" hope. It is a hope in a certain fulfillment of God's promissory history, in history, before the end of history.

Chiliastic hope does not exclude eschatological hope but rather belongs to it if in contrast to chiliastic hope one understands eschatological hope as the expectation of the end of the world, of the universal resurrection, of judgment, and of eternal life. It represents neither a transformation of eschatology into utopia nor a secularization of Christian hope. Chiliasm is the side of eschatology turned toward history. Eschatology is the side of history turned toward the life beyond. One can thus venture this thesis: There is no eschatology without chiliasm and no chiliasm without eschatology.

It is astonishing and worthy of consideration that Christians have had a positive relationship to Israel and the Jews when this chiliastic aspect of their hope was alive. A lack of relationship to Israel and the Jewish hope developed only when chiliasm was declared heretical. In truth, however, there is no Christian eschatology without Israel. C. A. Auberlen said correctly in the nineteenth century, "We shrug our shoulders about the elected people, therefore also about chiliasm."[11]

Why was chiliasm banned from the Christian eschatology of the church? The Lutheran Augsburg Confession declares in Article 17, "Rejected, too, are certain Jewish teachings (*Judaicae opiniones*) which are even now making an appearance and which teach that, before the resurrection of the dead, saints and godly men will possess a worldly kingdom and annihilate all the godless." The Reformed *confessio Helvitica Posterior* of 1566 said much the same thing in Article 11: "We condemn as well the Jewish dream (*Judaica somnia*) that, at the last judgment a golden age (*seculum aureum*) will come on earth and the pious will take hold of the riches of the world."

Why are "Jewish teachings and dreams" mentioned here? This has its roots not only in the messianic movements in European Judaism of the Reformation period and their influence upon the Anabaptist movements and the liberation struggle of the peasants. There is also within it a judgment of the Jewish hope itself—the condemnation of it as "worldly," "secular," and "fleshly." This theological judgment, though, is basically politically motivated: The "thousand-year reign" of Christ on earth places the right of political rule of the powerful in question, especially if with this hope is expected the abolishment of all rule, domination, and violence. The Jewish hope in the Messiah was viewed as a political danger in Christian lands. The surrendering of this hope was always the precondition for the acceptance and assimilation of the Jews. Christian communities which promulgated chiliastic hope were also persecuted by Christian and non-Christian rulers.

Yet when the chiliastic hope in the messianic kingdom is rejected, what steps into its place? It is worthy of note that in Christian history it was not another hope but rather, again and again, the present fulfillment of the chiliastic hope which was put in its place.

1. The empire of Constantine was considered by many Christian theologians the "holy empire," the "thousand-year kingdom," in which persecuted Christians finally ruled in the name of

Christ over their enemies. This first Christian notion of empire had clearly recognizable chiliastic consequences. In the kingdom of Christ the church and state fall together. The nationalization of Christianity succeeded in the Constantinian empire. In the empire of Christ, the true Christians rule with Christ over the enemies of Christ. The persecution of dissidents as "heretics," pagans as "idolators," and Jews as "enemies of Christ" set the tone for the laws of the emperors Theodosius and Justinian. In the empire of Christ, Satan is bound; the Christian empire is the empire of peace. When the Christian state understands itself as the "kingdom of Christ" on earth, it understands itself in chiliastic terms with all the consequences which have been mentioned.

2. Since Tyconius and Augustine, church history has been continually chiliastically interpreted; the "thousand-year reign" of Christ begins with Christ's ascension and is identical with the empire of the church. The church is the kingdom of God on earth. This is to be sure a spiritual interpretation of chiliasm, for the resurrection of the just is to occur already in baptism. But the consequences in the triumph over all enemies remain the same: The Jewish laws of the Fourth Lateran Council under Pope Innocent III outdo the Jewish laws of Emperor Justinian in discrimination and degradation of the "enemies of Christ." On Luther's relation to these matters one is silenced out of shame. The church is the lordship of Christ, not yet the "kingdom of God." If the church understands itself as the kingdom of God, it understands itself chiliastically with all the well-known consequences for its enemies.

3. It is no coincidence that National Socialism, like Fascism, occurred as a "political messianism" and that the "final solution" to the Jewish question followed in the name of its Thousand-Year Reich.

If the church identifies itself with the chiliastic kingdom of God, an unhappy triumphalism emerges in it. It becomes triumphalistic in claiming to represent exclusively the kingdom of God on earth. It becomes triumphalistic through impatience with dissidents and critics. It becomes triumphalistic in claiming to be the fulfillment of Israel's hope. This is an unhappy delusion because it raises a chiliastic claim which must remain unfulfilled in history. Christian hatred of the "stubborn Jews," declared to be the "enemies of Christ," is grounded ultimately in the self-hatred of Christians on account of the impossibility of their own absolute claims, a hatred against the imperfectness and unrealizable nature of these claims. Christian hatred of Jews was seen correctly by Franz Rosenzweig as the projected self-hatred of Christians. This self-hatred develops out of the chiliastic overburdening of their own existence.

If, on the other hand, Christian hope is reduced to otherworldly and eternal hope, there can be two possible explanations. First it can be grounded in disappointment in the real future hope. Such a transformation follows upon disappointed expectations. In the second place it can also be rooted in the chiliastic interpretation of the present. Viewed from the perspective of the thousand-year reign, only the eschatological "last things" remain ahead: the world's end, judgment, and the kingdom of God.

From this one should draw the conclusion that it is theologically justified to place chiliasm wholly in hope in the future and so bind it with eschatology that no historical present, not even as yet the messianic time, can be interpreted chiliastically.

Only in Christian communities which have rediscovered chiliasm as a necessary aspect of Christian hope is there animated a hope for the future of the Jews, and that precisely in the form of a messianic restitution of Israel. The Dutch Federalist theologians such as Campegius Vitringa; Pietists such as Philipp Jakob Spener, Johann Albrecht Bengel, and Friedrich Ötinger; and nineteenth-century Lutherans such as Franz Delitzsch and Chr. Ernst Luthardt, as well as Chr. von Hoffmann, discovered the special meaning of Israel in the history of God with the world. They were all missionary theologians as well, for from the beginning of the end time they expected a blossoming of missions among the nations and the return to Israel. Their argument took this shape: Just as, from the perspective of Jewish-Christians, the mission to the Gentiles developed out of the rejection of the gospel by Israel as a whole, so at one time will Israel find its Messiah when all the Gentiles are brought in. The order of hope of the Old Testament prophets was first the Jews and then the Gentiles.

When Zion is restored, *then* the Gentiles will make pilgrimage to Zion in order to receive the law and justice of God. The apostolic order of hope is exactly the opposite: First the Gentiles and then the Jews. Once the gospel has won the fullness of the Gentiles, *then* Israel will be blessed. The last, the Gentiles, will be the first. The first, the Jews, will be the last; yet they will not be forgotten. The apostle Paul's mission to the nations was nothing other than a giant detour toward the salvation of Israel.[12]

Israel's salvation is thus the indirect purpose of every Christian mission to the nations. Precisely for this reason mission (in the sense of this mission to the nations) cannot be aimed at Israel itself. In an indirect way the mission to the Gentiles will "provoke" Israel to faith. If this is then the promise upon which the Christian mission rests, the messianic calling of Gentiles to community with Christ will in the end be completed by the Jews. It is not that they will finally become Christians or that Christians will finally become Jews but that each will be redeemed from their particular histories by the rule of Messiah.

Christians hope in the Parousia of Christ for the establishment of his kingdom. They have attempted to localize the place of his return in various cities. For the communities of chiliastic hope, Jerusalem was and is the place of the future appearance of Christ in glory. Important for the present and for the commission in history is the hope for a future of the Messiah which will be clearly both Jewish and Christian *in common*. Consequently, it must be stressed that also for Christians God remains faithful to God's promises to Israel and will fulfill them in God's kingdom. It is a further consequence that Christians will not come into the salvation of the kingdom of God without the Jews. Finally, it follows that without Jews, Christians in history cannot be themselves, namely, Christians.

Community on the Way

If, according to this Christian understanding, Israel has a special calling from God alongside the church until the end, what does it look like and of what does it consist? Federalist theologians and the theologians of salvation history have given little thought to this. Moreover, these two traditions differ between the recognition of a unique Jewish way of salvation and the simple belief in the faithfulness of God to Israel.

According to scriptural linguistic usage, election always intended a commission to a specific service in the world and in history. With this nothing is yet said about salvation or the lack of it in eternity. Whoever is chosen is commissioned to a specific service as prophet, priest, or king. The "chosen people" is by no means a better people than the other peoples. Nor does it become a better people through its election. The chosen people is nothing more and nothing less than the commissioned people, a people determined by its service to other people. No privileges which could occasion self-righteousness and haughtiness arise from its election. Since the divine commission to the people and the prophets led rather into conflicts which brought suffering, persecution, and death, it was experienced much less as grace than as a heavy burden. The prophets did not feel themselves "made fortunate," privileged, or elevated through their election. Rather, they desperately fought against it until the divine election overpowered them. It is a Christian misunderstanding of the election of Israel when haughtiness, certainty of salvation, and suspicion of others are immediately connected with it. With the recognition of the election of Israel, nothing is said about the salvation or condemnation of the Jews. This decision remains the province of God's judgment.

For what is Israel elected and called? Israel is called to the witness of the Lord to the nations. This call remains, for the Lord stands by the Lord's Word and remains faithful to the Lord's promises. But does this professed faithfulness of God to Israel include an empirical state of affairs? Many Christians gladly point to the sheer existence of Israel, threatened on so many sides, and to the astonishing survival of the Jews through the centuries of persecution. They would consider this something like a "proof of God." But this does not suffice. Gypsies have also survived for a long time in Europe. Something must follow out of this beyond the mere recognition of Israel's existence. One must also recognize and confess in what subjective and empirical sense the Jews exist and seek to fulfill their calling as the Israel of God.

1. The hallowing of the Lord's name must be mentioned first as a special calling of this people: "This calling makes the life and prayer of the Jewish people a blessing for all the peoples of the earth."[13] The public confession of the one God and the proclamation of God's holy name liberate the nations from idolatry and fear of demons. This liberation is also the object of messianic hope; in the messianic time idolatry and fear of demons will disappear from the face of the earth. The earth will be freed to be God's good creation. With the hallowing of the name of the Lord, the liberation of the earth has already begun.

2. The living, because experienced, hope for the kingdom of God must also be mentioned as a special calling of this people. Israel was and is the people of hope par excellence. Through Israel the sense of hope has come into the world of eternal repetitions. Hope is no longer an evil in Pandora's box as it was for the Greeks, nor is it a futile pain in the mysteries of the Maya, as in India. Judaism is certainly to be looked upon as the first and the original messianic religion.

Life in hope for the future of God obviously cuts two ways: Hope sharpens suffering from the injustice of this world and from the pain of the godless inhumanity of human beings, yet it also gives the strength to struggle for right and justice and never to acquiesce in enmity and strife. Hope in the kingdom of God makes persons capable of suffering and ready for the future.

3. Finally, the doing of the divine will according to the teachings of God's covenant also belongs to the special calling of this people—to establish justice and righteousness for all, above all for the poor and oppressed in human society, and to prepare the way for the promised peace among nations. It is false to see only "legality" and "works-holiness" in Jewish obedience to the law. There is dogmatism and works-righteousness everywhere. There are temptations which the righteous Jew has to overcome just as does the Christian. The coercion toward retribution and revenge often charged to Jewish faith in the law is totally un-Jewish. It

is an archaic law already broken through by the witness of the Scripture. The creative love which does not condemn but rather forgives and makes the unrighteous righteous is not the witness of the New Testament but of the Old Testament as well. Yet the Jewish religion finds its accent as a religion of doing. Through doing what is righteous, life is practically made holy. The message of Jesus is also full of indications of the necessary and self-evident doing of the will of God.

If we recognize and confess the special calling of Israel as the hallowing of the Name, hope in the kingdom, and the doing of the will of the Lord, then there is a surprising accord with the first three petitions of the Lord's Prayer which Jesus taught the disciples. This accord consists not only in words; it comes on the Jewish side from the spirit of the Torah and the prophets and on the Christian side from the gospel of Jesus Christ and the experience of the Spirit.

Is it not for Jews and Christians a tremendous surprise when they discover that they can together pray the "Our Father," to bind themselves to the hallowing of the Name, the future of the kingdom, and the doing of the will of the Lord? Christians would then, in their Sunday worship, pray the "Our Father" not only "with all Christians in the world," but also with all Jews in the world!

If one joins a community on the way through history into the future of God, then one must also know and acknowledge the differences within the community. As a Christian one cannot seek a better knowledge of the special calling of Israel without at the same time recognizing also the special calling of Christianity and perhaps grasping it more clearly than before. This mutual understanding is not a simple changing of sides. Jews do not have to understand Christians in order to grasp themselves as the Israel of God. But Christians must understand Jews in order to grasp themselves as the church of God. Jews can reach back to the history of Israel before the coming of Jesus Christ, but for Christians there is no history without the Jews. Therefore, there is understandably more significance in Judaism for Christianity than in Christianity for Judaism.

Considering the calling of Israel, what kind of call does Christianity recognize for itself?

From what has preceded it is clear that the church is not Israel's successor in salvation history, that it does not take Israel's place and does not take over Israel's inheritance. On the other hand, the church is not only a messianic revival movement within Israel, as the pure Jewish-Christian congregations around "the twelve apostles" originally understood themselves. What, then, is the church if it is not a phenomenon within Israel nor a replacement of Israel?

The church "of Jews and Gentiles," the people's church, is called to live out of the missionary gospel of Christ. It has its ground and essence in this missionary gospel. The internal ground for this gospel is the salvation of the world through the sacrifice of the Son Jesus by the Father. The external incentive for the worldwide proclamation of the gospel was the rejection by the whole of Israel without taking anything away from the Jewish-Christian congregations and the experience that the Spirit came to Gentiles without their having first to become Jews. Thus, the church is *grounded* in the sending, the sacrifice, and resurrection of Jesus Christ; is *occasioned* by the rejection of the gospel by the whole of Israel and its acceptance by the Gentiles; and is *directed* to the future of the messianic kingdom for Jews and Christians.

Christian theologians have therefore seen the essence of the church of Christ in the movement of the mission of the gospel of Christ to all peoples. This missionary sending is the particular commission of Christianity. Therefore true Christianity is to be grasped in this movement of messianic hope to the nations. All church institutions are, like the church itself, interim institutions, "institutions in transition" (W. D. Marsch), in transition to the coming kingdom.

Jewish theologians have seen the calling of the church in the *preparatio messianica* of the nations: "The religions coming out of Judaism have the task of preparing humanity for the biblically promised messianic era," said the French chief rabbi Jakob Kaplan.[14] He follows the medieval Jewish scholar Maimonides with this assessment.

In both of these definitions of the calling of the church, one can perceive a certain amount of agreement: Through the missionary church, Israel's hope comes into the whole world. And with the redeeming of the world, Israel shall also be redeemed. Therefore, the appearance of Christianity is a step toward the redemption of Israel and the world. The way of the gospel from Israel to the nations is, for the Jewish Apostle Paul, a way to Israel's benefit. The better Christianity fulfills its task of the "messianic preparation" of the nations and cultures, the more it will also "provoke" Israel to faith, as Paul suggests in Rom. 11:11, 14. This invitation clearly remains open to every Jew to participate in the messianic preparation of the nations through the gospel. Jewish Christians must not give up the promises to the Fathers and their Israelite hopes; I believe they are not permitted to do that. To be a Christian is a possibility and a calling at the beginning of the "messianic time." Therefore it is a calling and a possibility for everyone, for the Jew first and also for us Gentiles.

The Existence of the State of Israel

Whoever is acquainted with Israel theologically must know that, according to the promises to the Fathers, "God, people, and land belong together." In the time of the European Enlightenment, theologians and philosophers gladly distinguished between God and the Jewish people in order to take over Old Testament monotheism but no longer to regard the people. Today it is known that God and God's people belong in covenant together and thus cannot be separated from each other. Hence, today many theologians are ready to recognize the God of the covenant and God's people but want nothing to do with the promise of land to the people because that reaches into politics. This modern separation, however, is as impossible as the old one: Whoever recognizes the covenant of God with Israel must also take the promise of land in earnest. That does not mean that one must become a "Zionist." The promise of land is not unconflicted even among the Jews, and not every Jew is certain whether today the "time of the homecoming" has already begun. Still the promise of land remains. Christians have no right to deny it, and they must also certainly not become champions of its fulfillment in the present State of Israel. The business of the promise of land and the State of Israel is first the matter of the Jews. The following reflections, therefore, are meant only to contribute to the ongoing discussion and not to press in this or that direction.

The promise of land is a condition inseparable from the promises of Israel. But the claim to its fulfillment in historical time leads to an ambiguity: (1) Jewish existence can be lived whole, unestranged, and unrestructured only in their own land. Therefore, the people Israel need the land Israel. (2) Yet in their own land and state, Jewish existence comes under the economic, political, and military laws of peoples and nations. Economic expansion, capitalistic competition, the military laws of security, and, finally, compromising diplomatic alliances with dictatorial regimes of the Third World beset and darken Jewish existence.

Does Jewish existence in the land of Israel threaten non-Jewish Arab existence? The "political innocence" of a Judaism limited to a synagogal religious community has been given up in the foundation of the State of Israel in Palestine. Do political and military considerations force the nation of Israel to be a nation like all the others? Is the founding of the state in Palestine a sign of faithfulness to God or of the paganizing of Israel? How can Israel become "a blessing for all the nations" if it has become a curse for oppressed Palestinians? Is Zionism the realization of the messianic hope of the Jews or its abandonment? Will the temple be built again in Jerusalem and sacrifices again brought there, or must one wait until the Messiah comes? Is it possible to think of a non-Zionist, Jewish existence and a non-anti-Jewish, Arab existence next to each other in Palestine? These are questions, but they are not questions to which Christians and especially Christians in Germany can give the right answers.

The basic theological question which lies behind them is, Is there to be a homecoming into the land Israel and the fulfillment of the promise of land already in historical time or only in messianic time? In which time do we live?

214

In one sense that is also a question of Christian existence: Can one live according to the Sermon on the Mount and also live politically? No state can be ruled according to the Sermon on the Mount, assumed Bismarck, the Christian. With the Sermon on the Mount no revolution can be made, thinks Herbert Marcuse, the atheist. As experience has taught, however, it was disastrous for us to attempt a revolution and build a state in opposition to the Sermon on the Mount. Yet when and how can Christian existence wholly be lived according to the Sermon on the Mount? Only "under the cross"?

In a deeper sense the political-theological problems of the State of Israel are also problems of Christians. There are not two peoples of God but rather only one people of God, because God is one. If the departure of Christianity from Judaism represents a first, enormous, and, in a certain sense, necessary schism, Jews and Christians nevertheless still belong to one people of God. In Christ we see not only true God and true human being but also Israel, that is, the firstborn of many brothers and sisters. Through Jesus we recognize Israel and are joined with Judaism, even though we must follow different callings. The separation from Judaism created the first ecumenical problem, which has existed for two thousand years; in community with Judaism the last ecumenical problem will also have to be solved.

Ecumene with Judaism can presently mean:

1. To read and understand the faith- and life-witnesses of Israel from the Scripture until today as the witnesses of the one people of God. Christian and Jewish exegesis belong together.

2. To share as Christians in the joys and sufferings of the State of Israel.

3. To know ourselves as Christians, together with Jews and Israelis, to be called to hope for the redeeming kingdom and to prepare for this kingdom through the liberation of all peoples. It is not for their own sake but rather to witness to the nations that Israel and church are called. Ecumenically this means: "the whole inhabited earth." For the masses of humanity, though, the world today is not habitable. Thus the common task of Jews and

Christians is to make the earth habitable for poor, hungry, oppressed people and with them to make the earth habitable for the Lord, as Psalm 24 says.

An old Jewish proverb says: "The Messiah will not come until all the guests are seated at the table." The Christian version of this proverb must be: "The Messiah Jesus has come, so that all guests may sit at the table." Thus, we prepare a table for the peoples and invite the guests of the Lord. Jewish-Christian *ecumene* could mean that already here and now.

NOTES

1. J. B. Metz, "Ökumene nach Auschwitz-Zum Verhältnis von Christen und Juden in Deutschland," in *Gott nach Auschwitz. Dimensionen des Massenmords am jüdischen Volk,* ed. E. Kogon (Freiburg, 1979), 126.

2. Cf. Jürgen Moltmann, "The Church and Israel," in *The Church in the Power of the Spirit,* trans. Margaret Kohl (New York: Harper and Row, 1977), 136–50; B. Klappert, "Israel und die Kirche: Erwägungen zur Israel lehre Karl Barths," *Theologische Existenz heute* 207 (1980); Rosemary R. Ruether, *Faith and Fratricide: The Theological Roots of Anti-Semitism* (New York: Seabury Press, 1974); Chr. Klein, *Theologie und Anti-Judaismus. Eine Studie zur deutschen theologischen Literatur der Gegenwart* (Munich, 1979).

3. Rudolf Bultmann, *Essays Philosophical and Theological* (London: SCM Press, 1955), 208.

4. P. Althaus, *Die letzten Dinge,* 7th ed. (Gütersloh, 1956), 313.

5. Ibid.

6. Thus G. Klein, "Individualgeschichte und Weltgeschichte," *Evangelische Theologie* 24 (1964), 126ff.

7. In the "Erwägungen zur kirchlichen Handreichung zur Erneuerung des Verhältnisses von Christen und Juden," Professors of the Theological Faculty of Bonn, *Der Weg* (August 3, 1980).

8. Ibid., no. 8.

9. Arnold A. van Ruler, *The Christian Church and the Old Testament,* trans. Geoffrey Bromiley (Grand Rapids: Wm. B. Eerdmans, 1971).

10. Cf. the detailed treatment of H. Bietenhard, *Das tausendjährige Reich. Eine biblisch-theologische Studie* (Zurich, 1955). For the political form of chiliasm see Norman Cohn, *The Pursuit of the Millennium:*

Revolutionary Messianism in Medieval and Reformation Europe, rev. ed. (New York: Oxford University Press, 1970).

11. C. A. Auberlen, quoted by P. Althaus, *Die letzten Dinge*, 306.

12. Ernst Käsemann, *New Testament Questions of Today* (Philadelphia: Fortress Press, 1969).

13. Cf. the Declaration of the French Bishops' Committee for Relations with Judaism on the stance of Christians to Judaism, April 1973.

14. In the Jewish response to the Declaration of the French Bishops, *Judaica* 29 (1972): 44ff.

INDEX

INDEX